Douglas

China Repairs & Restoration

China Repairs
& Restoration

by Rena Cross

Photography by Bruce Perry

LONDON

W. Foulsham & Co Ltd

NEW YORK TORONTO CAPE TOWN SYDNEY

W. FOULSHAM & CO LTD
Yeovil Road, Slough, Bucks, England

ISBN 0-572-00805-8

Printed in Great Britain by
Redwood Press Limited, Trowbridge, Wiltshire

Contents

Introduction 7

Chapter 1 Apprentice Exercises 11

Chapter 2 Means of Support 17

Chapter 3 Holes, Chips and Missing Pieces 27

Chapter 4 Cabinet Pieces 39

Chapter 5 Colouring and Finishing 51

Chapter 6 Repairing Dolls 57

Chapter 7 Miscellaneous Repairs 63

Chapter 8 Unexpected Bonuses 67

Chapter 9 Turning the Hobby to Profits 75

Introduction

THERE WAS A TIME, and not so long ago at that, when china repairs were undertaken by professionals at a proportionally small cost. Forty years ago, broken pieces were riveted at a penny a rivet, and although the result was unsightly, the rivet body showing on one side of the piece, it was permanent and completely waterproof.

Today riveting costs a small fortune, even if one can get it done, and is actually made unnecessary since the introduction of completely waterproof glues, particularly epoxy glues, which make possible an almost or completely invisible join as firm and durable as ever riveting could be. Thus one technological advance supercedes another, and although it is possible for an amateur to effect riveting, it is no longer necessary, and as a process requiring extra apparatus and some little practice, is of academic interest only.

However, if rivets can be placed in china and porcelain, they can also be removed, and this is well worth trying, because one often comes across a very desirable piece in an antique shop, disfigured by a line of metal rivets. The services of professional repairers are at a premium, and an antique dealer would often rather unload such a piece for a few shillings than commission an expensive repair which may lie in the repairer's shop for months.

Is it worth buying damaged pieces and restoring them? Most certainly. Naturally, however well repaired, a damaged piece never regains its original value, but as antique prices soar, the number of whole pieces decreases, because of all antiques, china and porcelain are the most easily damaged. Certainly the value of a damaged piece is enormously enhanced by the effecting of a skilful repair, and – let's face it – this is the only way many of us can become the owner of a piece of Bow or Chelsea.

Let's not overlook the utilitarian aspect of china repair, that of restoring modern domestic china to full every-day use. Good china is by no means cheap, and the first breaking of a piece from a dinner or tea-set is not only an inconvenience, but something of a psychological tragedy. (Women feel this especially. A broken plate or cup is more than a single smashed piece; it represents a violated set.) Chipped cups, and more especially tea-pot spouts have a sleazy look, not completely compatable with the gracious living image which is, to most of us, perpetually one step away.

How good should a china repair be? Ideally, it should stand up to reasonable scrutiny without being obvious. At best, a cursory glance should not reveal a mended break. The replacement of missing pieces, limbs, flowers, or boscage on a figurine should blend sufficiently well not to be obvious when the piece is on the mantlepiece or in a cabinet, and the observer standing a few yards away. It is quite possible to effect a completely invisible repair.

This standard of repair is perfectly feasible, depending on the severity of the damage, and the acquired skill of the repairer. One needs little more than a certain neat-fingeredness and a considerable amount of patience to repair simple single and multiple breaks, and some artistic ability and a good eye for colour when replacing patterns or missing pieces on figurines. In this latter exercise, considered by many people to be what china doctoring is all about, one often needs imagination, because there is no law compelling one to use conventional materials in repairs of this nature. If the effect can be better achieved by using a piece of carved wood, or a metal strip painted over with a certain skill, then these are obviously the materials to use. A china repair is in the nature of a *trompe d'oiel* anyway, and the result is more important than the material used.

One does not become a competent repairer in a day. But if one starts with the simple techniques, and progresses in stages to the more complicated, considerable skill can develop.

Tools and materials are necessary, of course, none of which need be particularly expensive. Because the immediate purchase of vast quantities of gear can put a damper on any do-it-yourself project (you often feel forced to justify the expenditure), we have prefaced each chapter with a list of the equipment needed for *those particular projects alone*. A complete list appears towards the end of the book.

But as soon as it appears likely that you are going to take up china repairing, make representation to your dentist (yes, your dentist), to buy certain second-hand instruments from him, the prices of which are rather prohibitive when new.

Beyond this, most of the required tools can be bought for a few pence, or are found in a domestic tool box. The appendix gives a list of suppliers of the materials you require.

In general, although china repairing needs fairly skilful fingers, some artistic talent and a good eye for colour, as an art and hobby it is in many ways easier than the repair and restoration of furniture. (See 'Furniture Doctoring and French Polishing, C. Harding'). In working with furniture, often there is only one way in which a process can be effected, and only one material that can be used, but when repairing china, there is a wide selection of method and material, so that a little experimentation will show how you can best suit your personal taste and mode of work.

If you follow the directions in this book, it is virtually impossible to fail in this fascinating art, and the result may well be a highly desirable collection of pieces at a very small cost.

To complete all processes outlined in Chapter 1, you will need the following tools and materials:

bland soap, soap powder or soft soap
plaster of Paris
plasticine
epoxy glue (Araldite is recommended)
low-melting-point paraffin wax or modelling wax

Any or all of these, as required

acetone (nail polish remover)
alcohol (methylated, surgical or white spirits)
lacquer thinner
carbon tetrachloride (dry cleaning fluid)

fine wire brush or steel wool
small square of glass or glazed tile

fine tweezers
small pointed tool
fine probe
small scalpel

NOTE   The last four impliments can be bought second-hand from your dentist (dentist willing), but the pointed tool can be satisfactorily made by taking a large needle, heating the eye-end, and inserting it into the end of a wooden skewer. It is then glued into position.

Chapter 1   Apprentice Exercises

ALMOST EVERY HOUSEHOLD can produce a rather nice cup or plate broken in the distant past, and glued together (usually badly out of alignment), with streaky globular glue, probably still smelling faintly of fish. If your nome is deficient in this matter, often a very nice damaged piece can be bought at a jumble sale for a few pence.

Obviously the first step is to remove the old glue, and since most of the old glues were water-soluble, it is often sufficient to soak the piece in warm water, using soft soap, or washing-up liquid. The very fact that previous generations worked on the principle that the more glue used, the better the join, acts in your favour, because as the glue softens, it is often possible to pull most of it out in a single strip with a pair of fine tweezers, or lift it off with the point of a fine tool or the tip of a knife or scalpel blade. If this is not effective, it is often a good idea to place your piece in a saucepan of cold water and gently boil it up, with the addition of soft soap or a bland liquid soap or soap powder *without* added bleaching agents or soda, when the expansion of the pieces may tear the break apart. But if the piece of delicately coloured, especially hand-painted, colour-fading may occur, and you must use your judgement about this.

However, if soap and water is not effective, most old glues will dissolve in a suitable solvent, including:
acetone (nail polish remover)
alcohol (methylated, surgical or white spirits)
lacquer thinners
carbon tetrachloride (dry cleaning fluid)

All these solvents are cheap and easy to obtain, and should be used with care, as they are all fire hazards, and all can produce fumes if used in a confined space. (China repairing brings one very close to one's work, and fumes can bring discomfort to the eyes, if nothing worse.)

If you use these solvents in succession, clean your piece well before trying the next on the list. Apply solvents freely with a swab, when, if you have hit on the right one, the joins will begin to loosen. Then soak well in the appropriate solvent.

Once you have got your piece (we'll consider a plate for the moment), back into its component parts, so to speak, all broken edges must be cleaned thoroughly and completely, not only of the remaining glue, but of dirt and grease as well. Pick away as much glue as possible, swab with your suitable solvent, or scrub with a fine wire brush or steel wool.

(If no solvent has been successful, you may be faced with a modern repair effected with epoxy glue, and it is at once the advantage and disadvantage of epoxy glues that once hardened, no solvent in the world will dissolve them. It is sometimes possible to pick away the glue bit by bit, but it is seldom worth the trouble. Strength of character is often judged in the ability to admit defeat, and this may be an occasion for that strength. Before it is completely set, epoxy glue can be removed with methylated spirits.)

Once you have your separate parts nicely and completely cleaned, your impulse will be to reach for the epoxy glue, to mix it according to instructions, and to get on with the job of mending.

But first . . . (every experienced do-it-yourself enthusiast knows this particular snag. Working from a book of instructions, you are ready to reach for your next implement, your next bottle or tin, and you read the words 'but first'). Well, better first than later.

Epoxy glue sets in twelve hours, and develops maximum strength in a week (quicker if heat is applied), and during this time, your mended pieces *must be kept absolutely and completely still*, without shifting a fraction of a millimeter. If the use of the wrong glue (and probably too much of it), was Mistake Number One in china repairing, the failure to keep the piece still and rigid is undoubtedly Mistake Number Two. Since you cannot stand for twelve hours holding a plate rigidly in position, a means must be found to keep it rigid on its own.

This matter of Supporting is so vital that we have devoted the whole of the next chapter to it, and you are strongly advised to read it *before* getting to the gluing stage in your first repair. Incorrect supporting, or the complete lack of it, ruins more potentially good china repairs than any other single factor.

Repairing a simple break

a) Mix epoxy glue on a square of glass or glazed tile, according to instructions.

b) Spread glue with the tip of knife blade or scalpel, or with the tip of your finger. Contrary to the old idea that the more glue used, the better the join, you are going to spread the thinnest possible smear of glue, as long as every part of the broken edges is covered. Scrape off excess if necessary. Not only will the thinnest smear give the best and tightest join, but thick glue-lines will push pieces apart very slightly. This displacement may seem infinitesimal, but when dealing with multi-breaks, the combination of a number of infinitesimal displacements may make an appreciable displacement at the edge of the plate.

c) Press broken edges together, and remove excess glue with methylated spirits on a cotton bud.

d) Re-align pieces if displaced.

e) Support the mended plate according to one of the methods outlined in the next chapter. Check when the plate is in the supported position that there are no 'steps', by running a probe lightly over the join in several places, first one way and then the other, and around the rim of the plate. Re-align if necessary, and recheck with the probe.

NOTE   Keep fingers and probe as free from glue as possible, cleaning them with methylated spirits when necessary. Nothing shifts china as quickly as gluey fingers.

f) When satisfied that alignment is perfect, leave the plate in the support for at least three, but not more than six hours. Thus the glue will be sufficiently set to hold the piece firmly into place, yet still malleable enough to be dissolved in methylated spirits if absolutely necessary. Twelve hours is the Point of No Return for epoxy glues.

g) Examine the plate carefully, swab off excess glue and probe the joint again. If alignment is not perfect (due to incorrect supporting), you may be able to break the join apart with the help of methylated spirits.

Repairing a multi-break
It is really surprising how badly damaged a piece can be neatly mended and restored to use. It is possible to use the simple gluing technique, working on not more than two pieces at a time, waiting until these are completely set before adding others. But, as in so many do-it-yourself exercises, a little additional preparation at the beginning will make the rest of the task easier, and we recommend the two following methods:

Wax moulds
When a piece is absolutely shattered, looking to the inexpert eye perfectly irreparable, there is a surprisingly easy method of effecting a repair, provided about one half of the piece remains intact, or you have a duplicate from which an identical mould can be made.

To make a wax mould
a) Buy modelling wax or low-melting point paraffin wax, the former from art-shops or school supply stores, the latter from a chemist.

b) If using modelling wax, warm it slightly until just malleable. The paraffin wax can be kneaded in the hand, when it will soften sufficiently. It is easier

Fig 1 To deal with multi-breaks, difficult to support, a mould is made from an undamaged portion of the piece.

Fig 2 The mallability of wax allows the edge to be eased, for the insertion of broken pieces.

Fig 3 The wax mould has been moved to the broken end of the dish and the glued pieces placed into position.

to use, but the modelling wax sets harder. Roll your wax out to half an inch thickness.

c) Cut a slab somewhat larger than the broken section, and press it under the *unbroken* section (or similar piece), until it takes on the required shape. (When working with cups, bowls etc, you can take internal moulds, which are easier to work with.)

d) When the mould is quite set, loosen it off carefully, and transfer it to the repair site, taping it into position if necessary.

e) Assemble the broken pieces into the mould, gluing them a few at a time, and allowing them to dry before proceeding with further pieces. Supporting is not necessary, as the mould will act as the support.

Plaster moulds

A mould made with Plaster of Paris is somewhat stronger, but when making internal moulds, it is as well to ensure that it will slip out easily. Where a wax mould can be warmed slightly to give it flexibility, and then carefully re-shaped, a plaster mould has no 'give', and may break. This is particularly important when your repair piece narrows at the top.

a) Mix a small quantity of Plaster of Paris with water to a stiff but pourable consistency. (Make sure that the plaster is fresh, i.e. white in colour. Greyish plaster is stale, and may not have the required cohesive quality.)

b) Smear the undamaged part of the repair piece with oil or vaseline, over a slightly larger area than the damaged site.

c) Have your 'prototype site' uppermost, and slowly pour over the plaster, covering foot, or base if they are present. Continue pouring until at least a quarter inch layer covers the site.

d) Allow to dry. When completely set, slide the plaster cast round to cover the repair-site, and secure it with sticky tape.

e) Place the broken pieces in their correct place within the mould, gluing a few in place at a time.

f) If you are repairing a plate, the mould will constitute sufficient support, but if mending a cup or bowl, it may have to be tilted to prevent the replaced pieces displacing either outwards or inwards, according to whether you are using an inside or outside mould. (See next chapter.)

Replacing cup handles

Where the cup-handle is intact, but broken off, the technique of cleaning and gluing are identical with those on page 11, the only variant being the need for correct positioning the cup to make sure the glued part remains perfectly still.

Repairing cracks

A wide lateral crack can be carefully cleaned of all traces of grease and dirt, and epoxy glue inserted, partly set, and the excess swabbed away with methylated spirits. The plate should be supported by the nail-and-rubber band technique, to bring the edges as close together as possible. (See page 19.)

However, it is often better to extend the crack to break the piece completely in half. If this cannot be done manually, a small pointed tool should be placed in the crack, and, once opened, a small wedge-ended tool (a chisel or screw-driver), is pushed along the crack until it separates the parts.

This opening technique can be used when gluing smaller cracks.

To complete all the processes outlined in Chapter 2, you will need the following tools and materials:

plaster of paris
plasticine
modelling wax or low-melting-point paraffin wax

sand-bed – shallow box filled with sand
clothes pegs
piece of wood, if you don't have a work bench
4 slender nails
stout rubber bands
hammer
supporting rods (dowels, pencils etc.)
very small sandbags or teabags filled with sand
stout thread or dental floss
box, tin or wooden block
strips of wooden lath or stout cardboard

Chapter 2   Means of Support

IN DISCUSSING the various methods of supporting your newly glued pieces, we must first deal with theory, because there are so many different types of repair needing different supports, and so many ways of making the required supports, that anything approaching a comprehensive covering of the subject would fill this book, and many more.

A glued piece must be supported so that the glued edges will stay in exactly the correct position until the glue is set, and this means that it must not move by so much as a millimeter, or the mended edges will over-ride, and you will get a 'step', or they will slip apart.

Fairly obviously, no glued piece is going to stay absolutely in place by itself, since the force of gravity and the fluidity of the glue are against it doing so. You have to construct supports in such a way that these forces are overcome. They will vary, of course, with the type of piece to be supported, and often with the angle of the actual break, since oblique breaks are usually easier to support than right-angle breaks.

However, one doesn't have to be a mathematician to understand this branch of the china repairer's art. Until experience helps you develop a supporting sixth sense, the following rule of thumb will help . . . there is a position in which the glued-on part of almost every china piece will stay in place without support, even if only for a few seconds, and this is the position which must be maintained by supports.

Because no two china repairs are exactly alike, there is very little virtue in constructing permanent supports. One can usually contrive from articles around the home, but a certain amount of material will almost always be in use, which it is as well to have on hand.

Sand-bed
The sand-bed is one of the simplest and most useful forms of support, comprising a box about three or four inches deep, filled with sand. In this articles for drying can be tilted at the required angle, and pushed down into the sand, where they will remain in position until dry.

Supporting plates and other flat pieces
a) In dealing with simple breaks, it is often sufficient to embed the undamaged

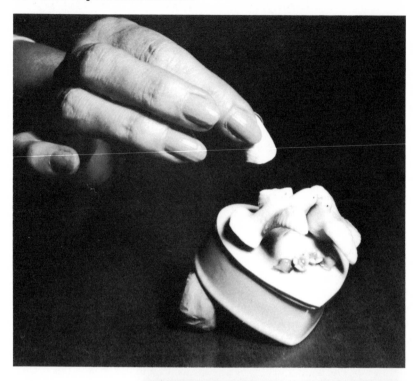

Fig 4   The test of correct supporting is that the broken piece should remain in position by itself for a short space of time.

Fig 5   The correct angle of support was achieved by altering the height and position of the plasticine. The broken wing in the picture remained in position without gluing, showing that the angle of support was absolutely correct.

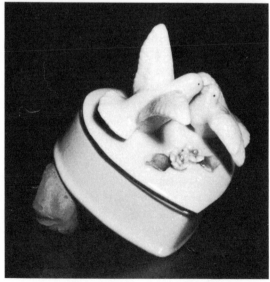

edge of the plate in the sand-bed. An ordinary clothes peg can be used to clamp the rim-edges of the glued repair.

b) Another easy method when supporting a flat piece – carefully shut the undamaged edge into the top of a shallow drawer, so that it is firmly caught. The bottom edge of the plate can stand on a box or other object inside the drawer if necessary. Clothes pegs can be used with this method.

c) A good way of dealing with multi-breaks in flat china – lay your unglued pieces in position face downwards on your work-bench, or on a piece of wood slightly larger than your repair-piece. Take two pairs of slender nails, and drive each pair in lightly opposite each other at right-angles to the break, the bases just touching the rim of the repair-piece, and the tops slanting well outwards. Remove your china for gluing, and then replace between the nails, stretching strong rubber bands between the pairs of nails to keep the mended piece in position.

More nails can be used if necessary, and the positioning of the nails altered to achieve the correct amount of stress without causing over-riding. In time, this knowledge becomes instinctive.

Cups, bowls, and other hollow-ware
a) These pieces usually need to be rested at an angle to maintain an immovable

Fig 6   A sand-bed in use. A sand-bed can be made to any required size, but seldom need to be deeper than this one, made from an empty chocolate box.

Fig 7   A newly glued saucer rests securely in a carefully closed drawer.

Fig 8   The nail and rubber band type of support. In this case, two rubber bands were not enough to hold the glued pieces steadily enough to prevent the edges from shifting.

position. It is often sufficient to place them in your sand-bed, but care must be taken to ensure that you don't get sand on the glue, or you will be in real trouble.

b) An equally simple support can be constructed by making two or more knobs of plasticine, laying the piece on its side, and pressing the plasticine into position so as to keep the piece immovable. (Fig. 10)

c) A hollow piece, especially a tall piece, such as a vase, can usually be supported by a series of dowel rods or pencils topped with a knob of plasticine which press against the side of the piece itself. If the bottom end of the rods tend to slip, they can be placed inside egg-cups or similar. This is a good method to use if your piece must be supported at an angle, when some supporting rods will be shorter than others. These rod supports can be embedded in the sand-bed, in which case the egg cups are unnecessary.

Handles, ears and figurine parts
Sometimes glued handles, ornamental ears and the limbs of figurines seem disinclined to remain in position in spite of angle-supporting, and can almost always be kept rigid by the use of small sand-bags or bags of lead shot. These bags can be made of any cotton material, and attached by means of stout thread

Fig 9 Additional rubber bands held the pieces completely steady. This is an easy form of support for flat pieces, if the requisite number of rubber bands is used.

Fig 10 The simplest possible support ... knobs of a plasticine keep this cup in position while the glued handle dries.

Fig 11 Prop supports to keep a drying piece at the required angle. The shortening of the props on one side determine the angle at which the piece rests.

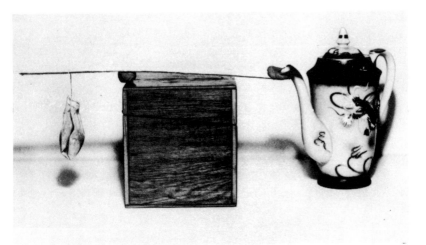

Fig 12   A simple fulcrum support for a repaired coffee-pot lower lip. There are many forms of fulcrum support made on a variation of this principle.

(dental floss is excellent), while two sand-bags used as counterweights obviate the need for tying the thread onto the piece, often a fiddly irritating job.

The sand-bag need not exceed two inches square, which makes it about the size of a tea-bag. In fact, an empty tea-bag is a time-saver, and quite strong enough for the job.

Sometimes a combination of angling and sand-bagging is necessary. A little trial and error is necessary.

Awkward and unusual breaks
While most repairs can be adequately supported by the means already described, there are always a few which obey no laws. While the art of supporting is involved with the use of whatever is nearest to hand and which suggests the likelihood of success, there are three techniques which will succeed in a great many cases.

Fulcrum supports
These are particularly useful in supporting a piece from *underneath*, especially in the case of broken lower lips of tea-pots, jugs etc. They are quite easy to construct, and there are many variations.

a) Take a box or tin, a little less in height than the site of the repair to be supported.

b) Place a knob of plasticine in the middle of it.

c) Take a narrow strip of lath or stout cardboard which exceeds in length the width of the box plus the distance between the box and repair-site. Lay it across the box, pressing it down onto the plasticine, so that one end of it rests *beneath* the repair. (Fig. 12)

d) Hang a sand-bag on the other end of the strip, and the weight of it will press the lath up sufficiently to keep the repaired piece in position.

This is the simplest, and often the most effective, form of fulcrum support, and there are many variations of it, built on the same principle. The only point to be remembered is that the upward thrust must be sufficient to keep the repaired piece in position, and not so strong as to cause the edges to over-ride. The pressure required is never very great.

Moulded supports

When a supporting job is obviously going to be a tricky one, rather than adding support to support to support, it is often better to consider the use of a moulded support, in the same way as a plaster splint is made for a broken human limb, and for exactly the same purpose. (One can often make a splint for the limb of a figurine in exactly the same way.) Obviously once a repaired piece is inside a mould of itself, movement of glued segments is quite impossible.

We dealt with the making of plaster 'self-moulds' earlier when talking about multi-breaks, and the same method can be applied when making moulded supports. This method is particularly effective when you have a right-angled break in slender pieces such as handles which turn out to be difficult to support effectively.

Thomas Pond, in his book, 'Mending and Restoring China' describes the supporting of a long-handled ladle with a centre break. He made a mould for the bowl of the ladle, which then laid at such an angle that the support of the handle presented no problem, being supported by two knobs of plasticine, one each side of the actual break.

Curiously enough, I was faced with the same problem in my early days of china repairing. (Ladle handles are notoriously difficult to repair.) I finally solved the problem by jamming the bowl of the ladle into the toe of a scuff slipper. It worked very efficiently, but the slipper was really never the same again.

Thus, in awarding Mr Pond full marks for technique, I do claim a few for ingenuity. Many good repairs are effected with unlikely apparatus, most of which can be found close at hand in the home.

Bridging supports

When repairing cup handles or 'arms akimbo' in figurines, where *two* glued sites must be kept in position simultaneously, the best support takes the form of a *plasticine column* from the centre of the glued piece to the nearest body surface.

Simply make a small plasticine column, and flatten the two ends, one around the 'flying' piece, and one other on the body. The plasticine is made to adhere by spreading out the flattened ends, and by, if necessary, wrapping it round the 'flying' piece. More than one column can be used if necessary, but care must be taken that no plasticine gets onto a still-wet glued join.

This technique is most often used when gluing a broken cup-handle, and when constructing new handles.

To complete all processes outlined in Chapter 3, you will need the following tools and materials:

powdered whiting
powdered zinc oxide
alum
linseed oil or clear varnish
household bleach
epoxy glue
Uhu glue
modelling wax or low-melting-point paraffin wax

Any or all of the following

porcelain fillers
epoxy putty (epoxy glue plus kaolin powder)
tooth-fillers
plaster of Paris and powdered gelatine
barbola

Indian muslin
scalpel or razor blade
sandpaper or wet-and-dry paper
pencil lead
stiff wire or brass nail
small file
abrasive wheel (optional)
sharp scissors
sharp knife
2 pairs small pliers

a drill (see Chapter 7)

Chapter 3 Holes, Chips and Missing Pieces

Multiple micro-holes

Even in the case of a simple break, you often find tiny pieces missing. In actual fact, it is well worth saving even pin-head pieces, if they can be picked up, although there is nothing difficult in filling in small holes, because the external glazing can never be exactly duplicated.

To fill holes of any size, there are a number of materials called 'fillers', and you might like to experiment to find which suits you best. Out of the wide range of fillers, we have chosen six, as being easy to obtain and to use.

Fillers

a) *Epoxy putty:* made from a mixture of epoxy glue and Kaolin powder. It can be used if painted afterwards, as it has a rather dingy grey colour, but most repairs have to be painted over, anyway. Mix your epoxy glue according to instructions, on your glass or tile, and work in as much Kaolin as it will take. Mix in small quantities.

b) *Porcelain fillers:* sold under proprietary names for patching chipped bathroom fittings. Usually sold in tubes, it is easy and non-messy to use for this reason. Use according to instructions.

c) *Tooth-fillers:* especially the acrylics, for use on small fillings only. Expensive, but unshrinkable, and very efficacious.

d) *Plaster of Paris and powdered gelatin* in equal quantities, mixed with hot water. A traditional craftsman's recipe, and very economical.

e) *Barbola:* that malleable putty-like substance beloved of the artsy-crafty set.

f) *Gesso:* the constituents and use of which are detailed below.

Of all of these, Barbola will probably provide the best answer. Everyone who was young in the nineteen-thirties will remember the Barbola fad, when every naked box-lid or jar-top was encrusted with leaves and flowers made from Barbola, and then hand-painted. Many are still in existence today, and often find their way onto jumble sale stalls, proving not only that tastes veer away from flower-encrusted what-have-you's, but also that Barbola work has survived over forty years without crumbling to pieces.

Never buy too large a tin, as it tends to dry out, and softening it before use is a messy business. A piece of sponge-rubber glued into the lid and kept damp is a help, as is wrapping the whole tin, the lid tightly closed, in damp rags.

The techniques for using all the aforementioned fillers is basically the same.

a) Moisten the edges of the hole to be filled.

b) Insert a small quantity of filler into the hole, using a small probe or modelling tool, or the tip of a fine knife-blade. The size of the hole to be filled may guide you in choosing the size of the tool.

c) Press filler well down, over-filling rather than under-filling. Smooth off the surface, leaving it slightly above the surrounding surface. Carry the filler up onto the surrounding surface all round.

d) Allow to harden, and sand-paper smooth, and level with surrounding surface.

Large holes
Where a large section is missing from a piece, any of the materials listed above can be used, and if the piece is to be put back into every-day use, you may find epoxy putty very effective, as it has a high adhesive quality.

Use of epoxy putty
a) Mix your epoxy glue according to instructions, on your glass or tile, and work in enough Kaolin to make a putty-like consistency.

b) Proceed as above. If your hole is very large, make a little plaque of putty first, and then gently insert it into the site, the edges of which should be well-moistened.

Use of gesso
Gesso is simply equal quantities of fine (artists' grade) powdered whiting and powdered zinc oxide mixed thoroughly with any thin white glue, such as Uhu. It was once widely used to make the ornamentation on gilt picture frames and on certain types of furniture. It is also used in replacing figurine parts.

There are different varieties of Gesso, the above being the basic recipe, and we give two of them:

a) *Waterproof gesso.* A little alum added to the glue will make the Gesso waterproof. (As will, of course, the use of waterproof glue.)

b) *Flexible gesso.* The addition of half as much linseed oil as glue will give the Gesso flexibility, making it easier to work. Clear varnish will have the same effect, which is not unlike epoxy putty.

Backing for large-hole repairs

If you have some difficulty in filling a large hole, your task is made easier if you back the site of the hole with a piece of stout Indian muslin glued at the *back* of the china. This gives you something on which to build, and makes supporting during the drying process easier, if not unnecessary. If you are repairing a cabinet piece (see page 40) the muslin can be left in place, but if you intend to put the piece back into every-day use, make sure that you use an easily soluble glue so that the backing can be removed; certainly not epoxy glue, for instance.

Or once again, you can use a wax mould, as when drying-out glued fragments in the case of a multi-break.

Chips and shell-breaks

The edges of plates, cups and bowls are particularly susceptable to the loss of surface flakes, leaving an area often grooved like a scallop shell.

This can be a tricky repair to effect, and the choice of a filler is most important, as some fillers do not adhere well to such a wide surface, which means that an added adhesive must be used.

We recommend the use of epoxy putty.

a) Build up the missing surface in a succession of thin layers (the thinner the better), which smear off onto the unbroken surfaces.

b) Allow time for drying between each layer (Patience! Patience!) or you will drag off the previous layers.

c) Apply an excess of filler rather than end with a concavity.

d) Trim off excess filler with a scalpel or razor blade when almost hardened.

e) Allow to harden completely.

f) Rub surface with moistened wet-and-dry paper or ordinary sand-paper until *absolutely level* with the surrounding surface.

Use of wet-and-dry paper *(as an alternative to ordinary sand-paper)*

The use of wet-and-dry paper is considered faster and more efficient than that of ordinary sand-paper, and you may care to use it for this reason. Sand-papering can be a rather tedious operation, and one comes across rather a lot of it during china repairing.

Whichever you use, choose a coarse grade of paper, and cut off as small a piece as you can handle easily, fold it twice, and rub the required surface briskly, pressing down fairly hard.

To negotiate corners, and when smoothing repair edges, use the fold of the paper, refolding as the fold-edges wear off.

Avoid removing the pattern on the undamaged part of the piece. You will probably have to repaint part of the pattern in any case, and a little care in this respect will prevent you having to extend the job.

Coloured fillers

In practice, it is possible to add colouring to your fillers (see page 51) but since the most feasible types of filler have rather unfortunate colours of their own, usually grey, it is seldom a success.

It is usually best to use the most successful fillers, and resign yourself to painting over them.

Grooving for better purchase

To return to shell-breaks, the smoother the broken surface, the less likelihood of satisfactory adhesion. Grooves ground into the broken surface with an abrasive wheel or file will make your filler adhere better, and if you wish to develop extra expertise, you could construct a drill, similar to that once used to drill holes for riveting (page 69) which will make holes in which the filler can 'anchor' itself.

Always make sure that the broken edges are well moistened, especially if you are using a filler liable to shrinkage.

Building Up

Teapot Spouts are especially vulnerable, and broken, become a great source of annoyance. Even if you have the chipped pieces, it is often more satisfactory to build up a new spout tip. Before attempting this kind of repair, there are two steps to be taken:

a) Clean the spout meticulously, removing tannin stains with a solution of household bleach.

b) If the broken spout-tip is missing, and the original shape unknown, take thought before you start as to the type of spout you would like to have. Make a sketch or two, or examine similar tea-pots. In all events, don't start your repair before you have fully decided.

Although there are a number of materials you can use (listed on page 26) epoxy putty is again recommended, slightly drier than when used in flat-ware, because it is going to have to 'stand up for itself'. It loses some of its adhesive qualities when dry, therefore . . .

a) before adding Kaolin to the epoxy glue to make epoxy putty, put a stingy little smear of glue on the broken edge of the spout.

b) Add your kaolin to make a dryish putty.

c) Rub a small quantity of putty between the palms of your hands until you have a long thin roll.

d) Lay a piece of this putty roll along the broken edge of the lip, and draw a little of it back both over and under the edge of the remaining spout, to give it purchase.

e) Dip your finger and thumb in kaolin powder to prevent tearing, and draw the putty upwards and outwards into the pre-arranged shape. Trim with sharp scissors, after dipping the blades in kaolin, leaving the lip rather larger than the desired finished product.

f) If you have insufficient clay on the lip, add more to the centre, smoothing it in all directions.

g) Support the piece according to instructions in Chapter 2, **possibly with the spout uppermost,** as the moist putty would be displaced by a fulcrum-type support.

h) When the putty has completely set, it can first be pared, and then smoothed with sand-paper or wet-and-dry paper, both inside and out. When smoothing the inside lip, roll the paper around a pencil or wooden skewer.

i) Paint to match the rest of the teapot. (Page 51.)

Knobs, ears and handles. Occasionally you may find that the knob on a tea or coffee-pot lid, or the ears of a vase, have been so badly smashed that too much is destroyed for the pieces to be rejoined simply with a spot of epoxy glue. Or you may have a very nice pot with the knob missing, *and* a spare knob from a similar piece, but the broken edges bear no relation to each other whatsoever.

There are several ways of tackling these problems, and you will have to decide which is the most viable in your particular case.

a) Grind both surfaces level with sandpaper, and glue them together in the usual way.

b) If this method would reduce the shank or stem too much, build up one of them as you would a teapot spout. Grind down the site to which the build-up must adhere, and glue in the usual way.

Dowelling

If you feel that the foregoing may not constitute a strong enough repair, it is possible to use the technique known as 'dowelling', which is extremely useful when you have, for instance, a rather fine knob to a rather heavy lid, and extra strength is required.

Dowelling was in vogue when china was normally riveted, but although riveting has gone out of fashion, there are still cases when dowelling is still useful. It is also a good technique when replacing heads on figurines and statuettes, and when repairing dolls. It is only used when joining two solid pieces.

In dowelling, a hole is drilled in each of the two pieces to be joined, and a thin peg, usually of metal, goes from the base of one hole to the base of the other.

a) Ideally, this is again a job for the Chinese String Drill or other slow drill, and once you have drilled your tiny holes, the only ticklish part is lining up the two holes so exactly that they join without the slightest 'step' in any direction.

b) Where it looks as if the most careful measurement is not going to be the answer, drill your hole in one piece, and insert a piece of soft pencil lead, removed from its wooden casing, the point just protruding from the hole. Position the two pieces together carefully and rotate them slightly, so that the pencil marks the correct drilling site on the other piece.

c) Take a piece of stiff brass wire, or a headless brass nail, shorter and smaller in diameter than the depth and width of the two holes. Notch the wire or nail with a small file.

Fig 13 Section through repaired lid, showing dowel embedded in cement.

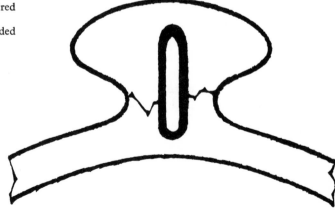

d) Partly fill your holes with filler (plaster of Paris mixed with water is quite adequate in this case), insert your dowel in one hole, and carefully cap it with the other piece. Wipe away any excess plaster and clean the surface.

e) If there is any chipping or flaking of the surface, this can be repaired after your dowel join is completely set. Touch up or repaint as necessary.

NOTE   A dedicated china repairer would do well to have a 'transplant bank' of knobs, handles, spouts and other parts. A great many good pieces can be saved by this method, but some knowledge of antiques is necessary if proportions are to be preserved. Public libraries usually carry a reasonable selection of books on the subject.

Creating new handles

A missing handle does not mean the end of the cup, and although the replacement is time-consuming and rather painstaking, it is well worth doing in a great number of cases. There are two methods you might like to try.

1] Moulding is used when you have a duplicate of the cup, or one similar. In the latter case, the repair is easier if both ends of the duplicate handle coincide with the sites of the missing one. If it does not, you are going to have to remove the handle-sites on the side of the cup completely, sand-papering them down, cementing them smooth, and painting them over when you paint the new handle.

a) Make two slabs of modelling wax or low-melting-point paraffin wax, longer and wider than the handle to be copied, and at least one inch thick.

b) Warm the cup handle slightly, and press it firmly into one mould, taking a good deep impression, deeper than half the diameter of the handle.

c) Repeat the process, taking an impression *from the other side of the handle.*

d) Lay a piece of notched brass wire bent into the handle-shape along one of the moulds.

e) Mix a cement of Plaster of Paris and gelatine, or Gesso, making it more fluid than that used for building-up. Lift the brass wire, and pour a little cement beneath it.

f) Put your two moulds together, and tape them in position. Seal one end with a knob of wax, and make sure that the other end is clear and open.

g) Pour in cement, and leave until almost set, but still malleable.

h) Separate moulds with a sharp knife, and remove handle.

Fig 14 The cup with the broken handle is one of a set, so a new handle can be constructed by the moulding method.

Fig 15 The first stage in making a wax mould from an existing handle, using low-melting-point paraffin wax, which is easily made malleable when worked in the hand.

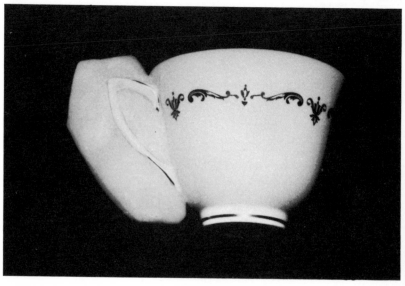

i) Examine handle for pits and holes, and if any are present, wet your finger and smooth the surface slightly and with great care, to prevent dragging off the cement. Pare off any excess with a razor blade.

j) Replace the handle in one half of the mould, as this will constitute a ready-made support.

k) When set rock-hard, remove it, and smooth it off with sand-paper, reducing it to the size of your duplicate handle if necessary. If pits and holes still exist when this is finished, they must be filled with the same material, left to set, and then smoothed off.

l) If stubs of the original handle exist, smooth the surfaces with sandpaper, and trim the handle to fit the stubs. If there are no stubs, simply smooth the sites with sandpaper.

m) Glue into position, and support until dry.

n) Paint as required.

NOTE In any kind of building-up, it is essential to make the part slightly larger than required, as it is far easier to grind down a part than to build it

Fig 16 The reverse mould is made in similar fashion. Both moulds are made fairly deep, and the newly made handle fined down to size.

Fig 17 The moulds are placed together and filled with liquid filler. After setting, they are separated.

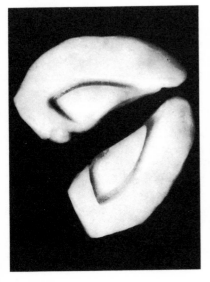

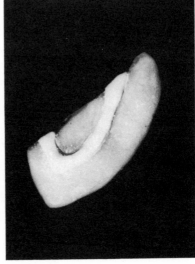

Fig 18   Four stages in
rebuilding a cup
handle.

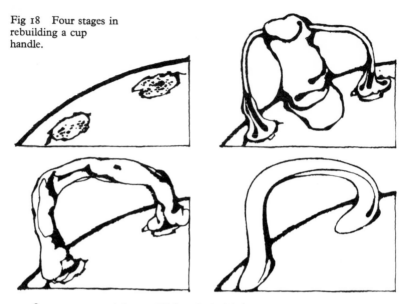

up after your material sets. This rule holds good, not only in this instance,
but whenever building-up is undertaken.

2] Building-up

This is a fairly long process, and it is as well to plan your supports before you
actually start your repair, because you will probably have to rest from time to
time. Your best course is to use your sand-bed, in which to rest your cup at
the correct angle (taking great care that you do not get sand onto your wet
cement), and a couple of sand-bags for use when your finished handle is
actually glued on. You can also use the 'plasticine column' technique to
support the glued handle, but not, of course, during the building-up
process, when the cement is not completely set.

a) Notch a piece of brass wire, and bend it into the required shape, using
two pairs of pliers if necessary. Mark the centre of stubs or old handle sites
with soft pencil, and cut the wire, still in its correct shape, to coincide with
them.

b) Using epoxy glue, put a small quantity on the stubs or sites, and at each
end of the wire.

c) Place wire in position, and make one or more plasticine column supports,
as necessary to keep the wire in position on the marked sites.

d) As the glue begins to run down the side of the cup, pull it up in threads with a probe to strengthen to join. Appearance isn't important at this stage, and a little roughness will help the final cohesion. The wire ends are covered all round with glue. Check the position of the wire at both ends, and put the piece away to dry.

e) When the glue is completely dry, check the success of your work by lifting the piece by the handle. If it doesn't hold, it's back to Square One.

f) Remove the plasticine support, cleaning it away carefully and completely. If handle stubs are present, scrape off the glue from around them.

g) Mix up a fairly stiff cement, or use Barbola. Since the handle is reinforced with the brass wire, the strength of the cement is not as important as it otherwise might be.

h) Add successive thin layers of cement or Barbola along the wire, and well down the ends onto the cup surface or down the stubs, allowing each layer to dry before adding the next.

i) When the wire is well covered, make a long thin roll of your cement, a little less than the thickness of your handle, because you have already built up a little, and have the thickness of the wire to take into consideration. Cut it to the required length, and roll it in a few drops of water.

j) Wet the covered wire with your fingers, and lay the cement roll along its length, pinching it into position, keeping your fingers damp. Work with extreme care, as the cement drags off easily. Fill in pits or holes with moistened cement, and trim off any great lumps with a razor blade. Don't smooth off at this stage.

k) Allow to dry to firmness, moisten the surface with a wet finger, and smooth out carefully. Fill in pits and holes with moistened cement, and make sure that the cement carries down over stubs if they exist, evenly and all round, or you will end up with 'steps'.

l) Allow the cement to set rock-hard, and again examine for pits, depressions and holes, which must be filled with cement. If your chosen cement has tended to shrink, stay with it, and compensate for the shrinkage with fresh cement. Many factors govern shrinkage, including freshness of ingredients, but a change of materials in the middle of a job creates problems best avoided.

m) When your handle is free of pits and holes, and again rock-hard, smooth off very carefully with sandpaper.

n) Paint as required.

To complete all the processes in Chapter 4, you will need the following tools and materials:

Epoxy glue
Uhu glue
liquid filler
plasticine
wax mould
paribar wax
Gesso or Barbola
Net or muslin
Cotton thread
Brass wire
lace or net
stiff paper, metal strip or brass wire
sandpaper

Small clamp
pliers
Drill

Chapter 4   Cabinet Pieces

A 'CABINET PIECE' can be defined as one of decorative value only, as opposed to one designed for everyday use. Although such pieces may include plates and cups and saucers, they are often of such value and delicacy that ordinary use is undesirable, and they are therefore kept on the mantelpiece or in a china cabinet.

This means that, although the pieces do not have to stand up to daily wear-and-tear, they have to be repaired in such a way that they stand up to fairly close scrutiny. If inquisitive friends insist on putting their noses right up to your repaired pieces, it will be probably obvious to them that repairs have been effected, but since they can be very good repairs indeed, this fact should bring nothing but astonished praise.

Actually, if you have followed this book, from the first repair of a single break in a flat plate to the building-up of a cup-handle, this chapter will have few surprises for you. You've done almost all of it before. You are conversant with the techniques of gluing, supporting, the choice and making of cement, of building-up, of filling in missing pieces, and of moulding. If there is something new to be learnt, it is simply that there are many materials besides cement for the effecting of repairs. We'll deal with that later.

Since we have dealt with the repair of flat pieces and of hollow-ware (and have the added advantage that cabinet pieces can always be backed with Indian muslin for added strength and ease of repair), this chapter is devoted to the repair of statuettes and figurines.

These are composed of solid parts and hollow parts, and the treatment of each is slightly different.

Hollow parts

A simple repair can be effected by carefully gluing the parts together, and by subsequently repairing any chipping on the join with cement, but the actual breakage gives you an opportunity to reinforce the part, and you might as well take advantage of it.

Reinforcement can take many forms. You can insert a roll of stiff paper, a strip of metal, or even a piece of brass wire bent like a hair-pin, cementing them in. If you mix a stiff cement and make a roll of it, one end can be inserted into one broken piece, and the other end into the other. The join is thoroughly cleaned of cement after the broken edges are placed together, and the piece put aside for drying. Extra gluing is seldom necessary, and missing chips can be replaced as previously described.

When a head is being replaced, cement should be smeared along the inside of the shoulders back and front, and a 'peg', reinforced with a thin metal strip or hair-pin-bent piece of brass wire, built up with cement over which the head can be fitted.

Indian muslin is, of course, another good type of reinforcement, and as its placement is to be permanent, plenty of glue can be used, preferably a thin type such as Uhu. The muslin is dipped in the glue, and inserted into the

Fig 19   This charming pair of figurines, now extensively damaged, were originally candlesticks for a Victorian child's bedroom.

piece when it becomes tacky. Smooth it in carefully with fingers or a small tool, and leave it to set.

If you are trying to reinforce an awkward piece where it is impossible to get inside a hollow piece, or are working on a solid piece, it is possible to make an outside reinforcement of a badly broken site. Dip a small bit of net or muslin in liquid filler and wrap a neat little bandage of it around the smashed wrist, neck or whatever. Tie with a minimum of cotton thread to hold it in position. When the cement sets, cover again with a thin layer of cement, allow to set, and smooth off with sand-paper. This is a good technique with difficult breaks, but the trick lies with a *thin* bandage and a *thin* cement layer, or your repair will look too clumsy.

Fig 20 The first stage in the reconstruction of the figurines. As a similar pair was not available, the missing parts were built up freehand.

Fig 21 The finished figurines, painted to match the original colours and completely reglazed.

Replacement

This is probably the height of the china repairer's art, and once you can replace missing parts for figurines and statuettes, you can consider yourself out of the amateur class. Choose the cement with which you feel most at home, because you are going to do free-hand modelling. If you would like advice on your choice, you may care to use Gesso, since it is flexible and does not shrink, but it is slow-setting, and therefore needs to be supported absolutely accurately. Barbola also has its place here, and is ready mixed, which is convenient.

a) If the part you are replacing is very small, such as a finger or the small part of a musical instrument etc, you can build it up, making it a little larger than necessary, then paring it down when the cement is almost set, and sand-

Fig 22   A side view of the figurines. The balloon sleeves on the boy's coat represent the fashion of the day.

papering when rock-hard. (The method is the same in essence as that used to rebuild a teapot spout.) Remember that paring-down is easier than building-up, and allow for this. If you have no idea of the size of the original, your sense of proportion must be your guide.

Paribar moulds

Small missing pieces can be duplicated in a mould made of paribar, a gum used by dentists for making moulds of teeth. It can be melted in hot water, but is not to be trusted to its own devices, because it liquifies fairly rapidly and can make an immovable toffee-like mess on the bottom of the saucepan.

Paribar is quick to use, hardening on about a minute, and makes a close mould if pressed well in. If removing it presents any difficulty, lever it gently with the tip of a hot knife blade.

Flexible moulds

When parts to be copied are of complicated construction, the removal of the mould may present a problem, and it is better to use flexible moulds, made from various rubbery substances bought from art shops and shops selling modellers' requisites.

b) Larger parts can be remade by means of a wax mould, in the same way as a new cup handle is made (page 33) as long as an opposite number is available. If you use a mould for a missing hand or foot, do remember not to give your figurine two rights or two lefts. Exact duplication of finger poses do not carry conviction, so try to vary hand poses a little. Moulds give a basic shape, and a little alteration to partly set cement will make satisfactory lefts and rights.

Working separately and working in situ

The decision as to whether you are going to mould your missing part separately or in its place on the figurine is influenced by a number of factors, including the hazards of the particular site (if they exist), and your own faith in your ability to make a reasonable duplicate at your first attempt. Of course, an unsatisfactory part can be removed, and the cement cleared off for another try, but this tends to be discouraging. In any case, we outline both techniques, and you must be the decider.

Working separately

If you are working on solid parts, you may be well advised to make your missing part off the figurine, as you will have nothing to work on, and you are going to have to carve away at soft cement with no more purchase than a smear of cement around the sides.

You can, however, build your part separately onto a piece of bent brass wire, and this will make the operation easier. Work with the loop of the wire at the top, and leave the two ends at the bottom free of cement for about half an inch.

Hold the wire ends in a small clamp, or embed them in plasticine, to leave both hands free for modelling. Cover all but the end of the wire with a lump of your chosen cement, roughly in the shape required. Moisten with a wet finger when required. Using small modelling tools, carve and shape the part to your satisfaction, ending up with it slightly larger than required. Leave it to set, but not to dry out, and then fill in pits and holes as you did when replacing a cup handle. When quite satisfied with it, sand-paper it smooth.

To replace it in its chosen site, drill a dowel hole in the correct position, place a little cement in the hole, and insert the wire ends, bringing the pieces together accurately. You will, of course, have to sandpaper the site smooth, and cut the brass wire to the correct length. Once a satisfactory join has been achieved, the two pieces can be glued together.

If the angle of the break is very acute, offering a comparatively large gluing area, it may be possible to dispense with the insertion of dowel ends into the piece itself, and they can be clipped short. But the loop of wire (or a straight piece if the missing part is very long and thin), make the task of modelling very much easier.

When repairing hollow-parts by this method, a dowel hole need not be drilled, of course, and the part is filled with cement into which the dowel ends are inserted. Take care to clean off any extruded cement.

Working in situ
Again this is easier if you have a dowel in place, either in the form of a loop or a single wire. In a solid part, the technique of drilling and cementing the dowel end is used, while a hollow part is filled with cement and the dowel inserted. In building up, the cement should be carried well down onto the undamaged area all round, as in the case of the cup-handle stubs. You build up and work exactly as you do when modelling the part separately from the piece, but you may be at some disadvantage because you cannot move the part so freely, and if you want to rest, you must support the whole piece with some considerable accuracy. You may also encounter difficulty in sand-papering your repair smooth, although this technique works quite well in parts which are not close to the main body, e.g. arms held away from the side etc.

Missing embeleshments
Often when a hand is missing, also missing is whatever the hand was holding. Sometimes one can guess at the missing part. A shepherdess would obviously be holding the traditional crook. A pair of musicians would each have a muscial instrument. Books on porcelain, or the owners of antique shops (who

are a kindly race of people), may show you a comparable piece, but where information is not forthcoming, imagination and your own particular sense of taste comes into play. A cornucopia may be more interesting than a bouquet. The hand of a court lady may be made to rest on the collar of an elegant dog. Look at pictures, look at other pieces, and when you make your decision, either make your model separately or build it up *in situ*, according to your inclination and skill.

Just because you are repairing a piece of china, there is no law that dictates that a replacement should be made out of china cement. The final product will be touched up with paint, anyway, and there are often far better materials for the purpose. A shepherdess's crook is a difficult thing to build out of cement, mostly because of supporting difficulties, although it can be done with the cup-handle technique. But it is far easier to make use of a smooth twig or a piece of fine piping bent into the correct shape. A musical instrument or basket in the hand of a figurine can often be easier carved out of balsa wood than built up with cement. The list of substitutions is endless, and in time the shape of a part suggests its own replacement material.

Backgrounds and boscages

Often a single figurine or group is backed by a plaque of vegetation and flowers, and often these are damaged. Where part remains, it is possible to copy leaves and flowers, and to build them up in stages.

These are best built up individually on your glass or tile, and Barbola is probably the easiest material to use. If the flowers are large enough, building them up petal by petal around a tiny centre will give them a more delicate appearance. If you make a centre first, and put a tiny ring of plasticine around it, you can curve each petal over the ring and onto the centre to give it a pretty appearance. (This is a chore, but the result is very gratifying.) Roll your Barbola out like pastry, cutting out your peta shapes, and moulding the edges a little with your fingers, place them over your ring, and let them dry hard.

Smaller flowers can be carved with modelling tools from a small lump of Barbola, using a magnifying glass on a stand if you need it. It is fiddling exasperating work, and we wish you the best of British luck! However, you won't get a good repair without good flowers – and the choice is up to you.

Where the background is simply an upright plaque, transfer flowers and leaves one by one, and glue them into position. Where the design calls for the remaking of trees or vines, these can be made of brass wire, bent as required, and branches, cross-pieces and twigs can be glued into position and supported in the sand-bed until dry. Glue one piece at a time, as you may need to tilt at an angle to prevent your tree from going out of shape.

When the glue is perfectly dry, and all cross-pieces in place, cover your tree with Barbola or cement. Dry again, and place your flowers and leaves into position. Dry again, and try the effect of the tree in its place in the group before you actually glue it into position. It is not always easy to judge composition and proportion.

It is also possible sometimes to replace your tree into the group, and to add the flowers and leaves after it is glued into position You can often get better composition this way, but the positioning of the rest of the group may make it difficult to glue in the leaves and flowers easily. Where there is a plaque at the back, supporting is usually easy. A knob of plasticine at the back will hold the plaque at the desired angle if it is laid down.

Broken lace

Many figurines are decorated with china lace skirts, which are particularly vulnerable. The remedy is surprisingly simple. Buy lace or net approximating in design that on the figurine, dip it in liquid cement, and as it begins to set, stand it up on edge, fluting it with damp fingers to imitate the folds of the existing material. Trim it with scissors when it is almost set, and glue it into position, overlapping the existing china lace on both sides. As a repair it may not stand very close scrutiny, but it makes a very good *trompe d'oeil* at a distance of a few yards.

Fig 23   The head and shoulder of this statuette have been glued into position, and the statue supported with plasticine for drying.

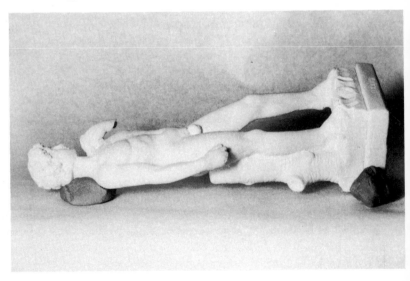

Fig 24   The glued neck join is still visible, some crumbling having occurred, because of the softness of the material.

Fig 25   A little liquid plaster is applied to the neck join with an artists' brush, to hide the join.

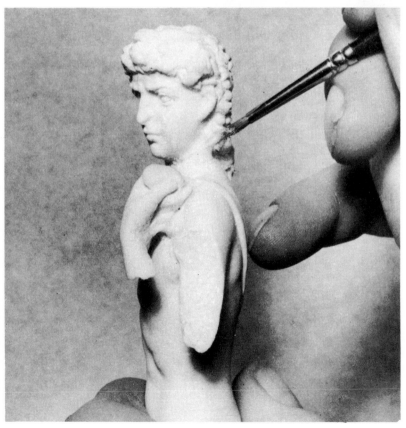

Fig 26   The arm of the statuette is missing, and has to be replaced. A fairly similar statuette being available, a wax mould will be made.

Fig 27   The rough cast in a wax mould, preparatory to being filed down before it is glued into place.

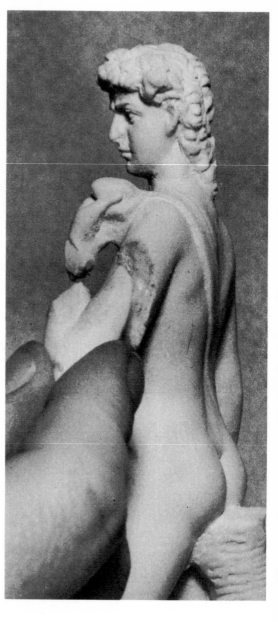

Fig 28   The arm is now ready to be glued into place. The statuette will once again be supported by knobs of plasticine.

Fig 29 The wrist must now be built up, and the fore arm fined down. The joins must be brushed with liquid plaster, and the neck join, now completely dry, must be lightly rebrushed with plaster.

Fig 30 The completely repaired statuette. Notice how the face and parts of the body have been brushed with liquid plaster where superficial damage had occured.

To complete all the processes in Chapter 5, you will need the following tools and materials:

All or any of the following:
Tubes of water colour
Casein tempera
Tubes of artists' oil colours
small tins of enamel and/or car touch-up paint
Gold paint, yellow and red, or American Treasure Gold
Gold leaf with special varnish
Shellac
White spirit
Stiff bristle brush
Soft brush
smoothing tool (toothbrush handle)

Powdered size
Picture varnish
Lacquer or polyurethane coating
Bronze powders
Amyl acetate
Permanent coloured inks

Tape measure
Tracing paper
Pencil
Scissors
Gold or steel nib

Chapter 5   Colouring and Finishing

OBVIOUSLY, once your repairs have been effected, if there has been any replacement at all, you are going to have to colour your repaired surface to match the rest of the piece, and probably to simulate the glaze as well.

There are a great number of colourants that can be used on porcelain and china, and their choice for any particular job is often purely a matter of personal preference. But, just as you may develop feelings of favouritism towards one type of cement, so you will grow to prefer one method of colouring above another. Unless you are conversant with the use of colour, it might be better to experiment a little with the following:

a) Water colour in tubes, which take particularly well when used with plaster fillers.

b) Tempera, especially casein tempera.

c) Artists' oil paints (buy small tubes)

When you use these three colour media, you will have to add a hard clear protective coating, not only to protect the colours you have applied, but to simulate the surface glaze that covers the original surface.

If you use enamel or car touch-up paint, they will dry sufficiently shiny to blend in with the surface of the glazed china. You will, of course, have to mix your colours to obtain the exact shades you want, no matter which medium you are using, and if you are striving for soft, rather difficult colours, you may do well to omit the car touch-up paint.

White can be especially tricky, because pure white, of the order of the Flake White you buy in tubes or in powder form, seldom exists in porcelain, and you may have to experiment to get the exact shade, usually by adding blue or yellow ochre. Try out with *small* quantities first, or you can use up a considerable amount of paint before you're satisfied.

In all events, no matter which type of colourant you choose, the texture must be such that it 'holds' sufficiently when you are painting, but doesn't drag at the brush as you're working. This is particularly important when painting on a curve, i.e. the side of a cup or bowl, when the paint is more likely to drain off.

Remember, too, to bring your colour up very lightly over the existing painted surface in a feathering motion, so that old and new colours blend, and there is no hard and visible line between them.

Choosing colours

In buying colours, it is best not to have too wide a selection, no matter which medium you use. You are unlikely to get a true colour match direct from bottle or tube, and will have to mix colours anyway, and to have more colours than you need is an unnecessary expense.

Obviously, in addition to white (of which you will probably use a great deal), you should buy the colours most often seen in china, and these will primarily be the earth colours, chrome yellow, yellow ochre, burnt sienna and Vandyke brown. These, mixed with white, will give you biege, biscuit, and most of the shades of brown. Grey is a complicated colour to mix, and is as well bought outright.

You will need the primary colours, red, yellow and blue, of course, but as you are more likely to use crimson than vermilion, rose madder is a time-saver. In dealing with blues, choose ultramarine as well as a clear pale blue, and a clear strong green which can be mixed with blue or yellow as required. You will also need black, but in small quantity, for line work, and in redrawing faces, hair etc on figurines.

Gilding

Perhaps this is the moment to talk about the replacement of gold, because gold bands and gold trim figure largely in the decoration of figurines and domestic china.

Use of gold paint

Gold paint is used in exactly the same way as any other paint, but varies considerably in tone, so it is as well to buy one small bottle of yellow gold and one of red gold from an art shop. A dark red undercoat enriches the tone of any gold paint.

The art shop may also stock American Treasure Gold, which is often used by antique dealers for restoring gilded picture frames. It is expensive, but can be rubbed on with the tip of the finger, which gives a smoother and closer finish than the use of a brush.

Use of gold leaf is a little tricky, but well worth trying, because the results are far better, and an antique piece of good quality is likely to have been gilded with gold leaf in the first place, so you will get a better match.

Gold leaf comes in a little book, not unlike a stamp book, each leaf backed by a piece of paper. It is applied with a special varnish, which you can buy when you buy your gold leaf itself. (If you can't get it from a wholesale chemist, an antique restorer may be able to help you).

Method

a) Seal the surface to be gilded with shellac thinned with alcohol.

b) Dry well, and apply several coats, drying each coat before proceeding.

c) Brush on the varnish, and while it is still tacky, press down the gold leaf, with the covering paper still on the *upper* surface.

d) Pat gently with a stiff-bristle brush, so that the leaf goes properly into any irregularities of surface.

e) When the gold leaf is adhering firmly, peel off the paper.

f) Pat the gold leaf with a softer brush, and smooth the surface very carefully.

g) Polish with a very smooth tool, such as a tooth-brush handle, until the surface is burnished to a degree that matches the gilding you are copying. (Special agate burnishers are available, and serve the purpose better, but the tooth-brush handle makes a very handy substitute.)

There is a snag to the use of gold leaf which no instruction book seems to tell you. Gold leaf is the most fly-away substance you are every likely to handle. (That's why it's back with paper.) Not only can it blow away in a draught, or fold over on itself, which is infinitely more irritating, but it can stick to your finger, and you are faced with the ridiculous situation of removing it from one finger to another, and then to a third. *Don't* remove backing paper until the leaf itself is firmly stuck in place, keep doors and windows closed, don't breathe directly onto the leaf, don't cough, and your chances of success are good.

Preparing a surface for colouring

We have previously said that, although it is possible to tint your filler, it is unlikely that you will get a good enough colour match to be able to dispense with surface painting. But a reasonable match may obviate a coat or two of paint, and you may care to try it for this reason.

No matter which colour medium you are using, even car touch-up paint, it is better to seal the surface of your filler, especially if you have used one of the plaster cements, which remain porous even when dry.

This is best done by using an additive to the paint itself, rather than by coating the surface before applying paint. This can be done by one of the following methods:

a) adding powdered size to the paint, in small quantities for water colours, more heavily for oil colours and enamels. (The ultimate test is the ability of the paint to remain on the repaired surface.)

b) adding a few drops of picture varnish (not any other kind), to your colourant, and mixing it carefully and thoroughly. Add a few drops of white spirit, and adjust colouring as necessary.

Test your colour by laying a few brush strokes along the undamaged surface. Remove them before they dry, using white spirit on a piece of rag.

Use good quality *clean* artists' brushes, possibly rather smaller than you might feel necessary.

Duplicating patterns
When you have completed your background painting to your satisfaction, and any depressions (which shouldn't really be there at this stage), filled in with paint, and a feathering overlap up onto undamaged surfaces, you are ready to copy the missing pattern.

You alone know your own artistic ability, and if you feel that you can copy a design freehand, you go ahead and do it, using one colour at a time, and allowing that colour to dry before applying another.

But if you are doubtful about this, you can easily make use of the following methods:

a) Measure out your design, using a flexible tape-measure if the surface is curved, draw it in pencil, and paint it in one colour at a time.

b) Make a series of stencils, one for each colour, by means of a series of tracing papers. Once you have made the tracings, make the stencils by cutting out the pattern for one colour, place it in position, and wash the appropriate colour over it. Make a tracing in this fashion for each colour in turn. Position your stencils carefully, and allow each colour to dry before applying the next.

NOTE It is important to duplicate not only a colour pattern, but the *depth* of the pattern. Where the pattern is raised, sufficient extra paint must be applied to raise the pattern to the desired height.

Where you have a very flat pattern, originally applied by transfers (as in Willow Pattern, and other Old English ware), duplicate the pattern with *permanent colour inks*, using a gold nib, or a steel nib annealed in a match or lighter flame, after smoothing the china surface with fine steel wool.

Glazing
Obviously, after you have duplicated your painted pattern, you must simulate the glaze, since it is not feasible to reglaze and refire the piece. The following methods will cover almost all the fields:

a) Any good quality lacquer or a polyurethane coating will serve. Apply with a very small brush, and feather up onto the undamaged surface. If you are dealing with a slightly coloured glaze, the blue-white of Delft, and the greenish or yellowish Chinese glazes, you will have to work a bit to duplicate the exact colours, using artists' oil paints, and adding lacquer to colour drop by drop until the right consistency is reached. When you are satisfied that your colour match is as good as you can make it, lay a very slight smear alongside your original glaze and allow it to dry, as you may get a colour change on drying, in which case you will have to adjust your colouring.

b) Colourless nail polish will make a good *white* glaze, but doesn't take to colouring particularly happily. (But worth experimentation.)

c) Lustre glazes can be simulated by mixing bronze powders with amyl acetate, but the coating must be very smooth and even, and of a brushable consistency. Curiously enough bronze powders come in a variety of colours, and can, at a pinch, be used for repairing torn gold leaf and disguising small gilding repairs.

d) The characteristic Beleek glaze can be duplicated very satisfactorily with white pearl nail polish.

NOTE If you use water-colours, particularly on a plaster filler, you may find their brightness reduced in value on application to the plaster. This happens particularly in reds, which may be reduced to dull brown. The colour is restored, apparently miraculously, after glazing, so the colour on the palette, and not on the plaster, should be considered to be true.

To complete all the processes in Chapter 6, you will need the following tools and materials:

Epoxy glue
Epoxy putty
Paraffin wax
Gesso
Flexible Gesso
Uhu glue or lacquer
Colourants

Elastic
Button-hook or crochet hook
Indian Muslin
piece of cork
Cardboard or metal foil
Doll's eyes if required
Round objects (marbles, ball-bearings etc), for making moulds
Knife blade suitable for heating
Artists' medium-sized brush

Plastic wood
Wood and woodworking tools

Chapter 6 Repairing Dolls

TIME WAS (again that melancholy phrase!) when every town of any size had a Doll's Hospital, and dolls could be professionally repaired at very little cost. Now one is hard put even to buy the necessities for doll transplant surgery, and one may have to search a little. It is often better to get directly into touch with manufacturers for information.

Antique dolls are a collector's item, and even the lush china-headed dolls made at the turn of the century are becoming highly prized, and will certainly accrue in value. A couple of dolls of this type represent a good way of introducing a little girl to the joys of collecting.

Although children are far less sentimental about their dolls than their grandmothers were, and although most of today's dolls are made of unbreakable composition, a reasonable knowledge of running repairs can make for a more peaceful household, and act as a re-affirmation in the belief that parents are still capable of making most things come right.

CHINA DOLLS

Broken heads

Even if you feel that you can mend the head satisfactorily *in situ*, you will probably do a more satisfactory and permanent repair if you separate head from body, the method of decapitation varying according to the type of doll.

Where the body is made of cloth or kidskin, the head will simply be stitched on through a hole in the china shoulders. If the doll is wholly ceramic, and jointed, the arms will probably be strung together with elastic, which can be cut, and the arms removed, so that you can reach into the inside of the neck, and unhook or unstring the head, according to the type of doll.

But . . . a warning. Restringing is not as easy as you might think, since most of the loops of elastic cross over inside the doll. The best plan is to draw a map of the internal workings *before* total dismemberment, no matter how ridiculous the suggestion might sound, or you may be in for a very frustrating time. In restringing, a button-hook is an indispensible tool; in the case of very small dolls, a crochet hook can be used.

The head should be mended according to the techniques already discussed with regard to the mending of vases etc, starting from the face and working backwards, so that final irregularities (if they occur) are hidened by the hair, whether real or painted. Reinforce the head by lining it with Indian muslin (page 40), or coat the inside of the whole head with Uhu glue or lacquer for extra stregth.

Replacing eyes
If the eyes are broken, one must, of course, mend them, and the head must be removed, whether it is broken or not. (If unbroken, you might as well reinforce it while you have the chance.)

If both eyes are damaged, the dimensions of the eye socket must be carefully measured, and sent to the wholesaler or manufacturer, because the eyes must fit perfectly, or the opening and closing mechanism will not work, or may scrape in the socket and work inefficiently.

If only one eye is damaged the replacement must exactly match the remaining eye, not only in dimensions, but in colour. It is often easiest to send the remaining eye with your order to the suppliers.

Repair the eye socket carefully, if it is damaged (Gesso does well for this job), smoothing off and sand-papering with great care, so that the eye will not scrape when opening and closing. When replacing eyes, coat the *outer* edge of each eyeball with paraffin wax for the same reason.

Eye mechanism
The opening-and-closing mechanism in an old-fashioned doll is nothing more than a lump of lead or possibly plaster in the centre of the eye-wire which is in the form of a T. (See figure 31). If this weight had become dislodged (and the eyes are fast open or fast closed), it can be simply glued back, but if it is missing, you will have to experiment a bit until you get the weight exactly right for a nice easy action.

Small balls at each end of the horizontal eye-join wire fit into sockets at the inner corner of each eye-ball, and if these are missing you will have to find substitutes of exactly the right size, or make them yourself from lead or other easily worked metal.

Replacing the eye unit
The whole eye unit can be replaced by anchoring it in place with epoxy glue or epoxy putty, after you have made sure that the eyes are in the right position in their sockets. Since supporting would constitute a difficult task, the whole unit can be held in place with lumps of wax, until the glue dries.

Most dolls have a piece of cork against which the bottom weight of the wire T-piece hits every time the doll opens or closes its eyes. Sometimes this cork

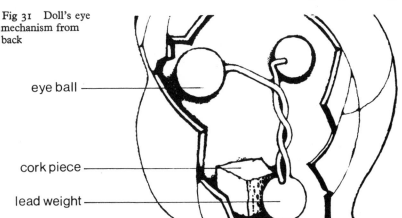

Fig 31 Doll's eye mechanism from back

eye ball

cork piece

lead weight

falls out, and the eyes move with a clacking sound. Continued absence of the cork will often cause the wire to bend (this should be checked on when you have the mechanism under repair), and it should be replaced in such a position that the weight will hit against it in every eye-movement.

Missing limbs

Solid limb dolls often have solid arms and legs, and like their hollow counterparts, are likely to break at the ball-and-socket joints.

a) Repair these joints by building up the socket with flexible Gesso or similar material.

b) When completely dry, smooth off and finish.

c) Make a wax or plaster mould of it for the reconstruction of the ball joint.

d) Lightly wax the socket on re-assembling the doll, for perfect mobility.
     Where breaks occur other than at the actual joints, it is best to use dowelling.

Hollow limbs

The technique for dealing with this is, of course, similar to that used for figurines, and the limb should be re-inforced with a roll of cardboard or of strong metal foil.

NOTE   Where joints contain hooks for restringing, these must be securely re-anchored if necessary. The hook-hole should be filled with glue or plaster, and the part supported until it is dry, with the hook in position. Where both round knee or both elbow joints are badly damaged, they can be recast from a mould of any round object (marble, ball-bearing etc), of the correct size.

Replacement of parts

A foot or hand etc, can easily be made from a cast of the remaining member, but if both are missing, you will have to take a cast from a doll of similar type. This is a job for one of the flexible moulds (page 43) although you can use low-melting-point paraffin wax, removing it while it still has a certain flexibility, but it is set enough to preserve its shape.

When casting, include a dowel or wire loop for reinforcement. Once the part is securely glued into position, it can be built up or fined down as required. If you prefer to work away from the doll, this is also quite viable. If you have done similar work on figurines, you will find doll repair comparatively easy, because of the greatly increased size.

The remarks with regard to lefts and rights, and to hand poses (page 43) also apply here.

Facial Surgery

Doll's noses are particularly accident-prone, and these are best remodelled from flexible Gesso on the face itself, carefully removed and set to dry, and when perfectly set, glued into position.

It is, of course, perfectly possible to build up a doll's nose in the same way as you built up a tea-pot spout or missing figurines parts, but noses can be surprisingly difficult, and it is amazing how much difference they can make to a doll's expression (doll's noses are almost invariably retroussé), and you may have to make a nose or two before you are satisfied.

Should you be lucky enough to obtain a portrait doll, i.e. one whose face is a facsimile of some historic personage (I once had one of the Empress Eugénie), it is well worth the trouble of a little research, so that it can be restored to its former likeness.

WOODEN DOLLS

Perhaps these do not come within the scope of a book on china repairs, but antique wooden dolls are becoming highly prized, and a little advice might not come amiss.

Where such a doll has broken joints, it is often better to make a completely new joint, and graft it in half-way down the limb, although the joint can be built up by means of successive thin layers of plastic wood, as one would use layers of cement filler to build up a shell break.

Broken joint tongues should *not* simply be glued into place, because this is seldom satisfactory. The stump should be slotted, and if necessary, a new tongue whittled and inserted.

Missing hands and feet can be carved out, and are usually easier to do than their porcelain counterparts. They should be dowelled into the stumps.

In painting an antique wooden doll, I personally think that a great deal of its charm is lost if it comes out with bright shining spit-new colours. Keeping to the original colours (if they are still apparent), one can get a pleasing antique effect by adding the appropriate earth colours, a touch of brown, amber or ochre, and by using light cream instead of white.

WAX DOLLS

The very creation of wax dolls was a tribute to the care lavished on toys by the children of previous generations. Although more pliable then than they appear now, age having made them brittle, they were extremely sensitive to heat and to over-handling, and must have been treated with the utmost delicacy to have survived until the present day.

Actually, their sensitivity to heat makes it possible for them to be repaired today, but this really is a technique which will test the skill and ingenuity of the best workman. Wax dolls are well worth collecting, but unfortunately repairing skill only comes with practise, and you may ruin a doll or two before you become expert. Unlike a china repair, which can often be stripped down for another try, a wax repair must be right first time, or it is a failure.

a) To effect a repair, first prepare paraffin wax by tinting it to the required shade with candle dyes, usually obtainable from handcraft shops.

b) Taking the two edges to be joined, *warm* one edge of one, and quickly run the flat side of a hot knife down the edge of the other, so that the wax melts slightly.

c) Press the warm and the hot edge together quickly, and hold at the correct angle until the wax sets.

d) This will only make a superficial join, which must be treated with great care so that it doesn't separate. Brush it over continuously with your melted tinted wax, using a medium-sized artists' paint brush.

e) When the join is smooth and sufficiently strong, smooth off with a heated knife.

On first reading, this sounds like a comparatively easy technique, but the trick lies in being able to gauge the temperature needed to just melt the wax, and the degree of warmth of the other wax edge, as hot wax will not bind to cold.

To complete all the processes outlined in Chapter 7, you will need the following tools and materials:

Plaster of Paris
Paraffin wax
Pure beeswax
Carnuba Wax
candle dyes
Sodium silicate
Ground glass
White oxide of zinc, tin or titanium
Sealing wax
lacquer
shellac or clear varnish
Epoxy glue
Epoxy putty
Gold paint or gold leaf
Gesso

Thick cardboard
Plastic wood

Small modelling tools
Small file or abrasive wheel
Nails and rubber bands for support

Chapter 7   Miscellaneous Repairs

THERE ARE a number of repairing techniques so closely allied to china restoration that they don't seem out of place in a book of this nature.

Gilt Picture Frames
The ornamentation on antique picture frames is usually made out of Gesso, and missing parts can be copied out of this material, either being built up or made in a mould. But before making replacements, examine the gluing around the whole frame, and take the opportunity of regluing any suspect pieces, or you will certainly have to do so later.

Chips and other blemishes can be repaired as you would a similar china repair.

Seal your Gesso repair with shellac or clear lacquer, and finish with matching gold paint (page 52) or cover with gold leaf.

Marble can best be cleaned with a solution oxalic acid, but care must be taken, as this substance is very poisonous. Wash down with the solution into a trough or basin, and then dry with a soft fluffy cloth.

Broken pieces can be joined with Araldite, and supported until dry. When repairing a flat slab, lay the glued slab on a flat surface covered with kitchen waxed paper, and put really heavy weights at both edges at right-angles to the glued join, so that the glued seam is kept in position. You can also use the nail technique (page 19) winding strong elastic or elastic thread around the nails if rubber bands won't stretch that far.

Marble being rather a friable material, there is bound to be a trough along the break-line, even after it is glued into position. Make a filler by mixing Plaster of Paris with melted paraffin wax, or preferably melted pure beeswax (the addition of a little carnuba wax will make it less brittle), and colouring the mixture with candle dyes if the marble itself is coloured. Veining can be painting in after the filler has set, to simulate the natural veining of the marble.

This filler can be moulded to replace missing parts if required. It can also be modelled with a warmed tool, but building up, which can be done by continually brushing on wax layers, is tedious and slow.

Where missing pieces are to be filled in, you can, alternatively, make a dough of sodium silicate and ground glass added to dry white oxide (the quantities vary according to the texture of the marble), which can be coloured with the addition of powdered pigments. Zinc, tin or titanium oxides can be used.

WARNING   Even if powdered glass is not a poisonous substance, it must be treated with the utmost respect, as even a few grains on a finger-tip conveyed to the mouth will result in quite incredible internal pain, and possibly severe illness, as the grains of glass actually lacerate the stomach and intestines.

Alabaster is repaired in the same way as marble, but as the shades of alabaster vary from pure white to dark brown, it is often possible to buy your beeswax in a matching colour.

Also do remember to melt beeswax slowly, preferably in a basin over a saucepan of boiling water. Beeswax is rather inflammable, and cannot safely be left to its own devices on the stove while you get on with other jobs.

Jade and Soapstone can be repaired by gluing with Araldite, after the broken surfaces have been roughened lightly with a file or abrasive wheel. The pieces must be clamped together as tightly as possible while drying. Dowelling can be used with advantage, as these substances are rather brittle.

If there are any pieces missing, and the methods mentioned above for repairing marble and alabaster do not offer a good match, sealing wax may well effect a good repair, if you can get a good colour match. Melt the wax into the required site, smoothing it out with any smooth metal tool heated above the melting point of the wax. (Experiment with this before trying it on the actual site.)

Lacquer Ware usually suffers from surface cracks, which can be filled in with carefully applied lacquer. Or you can apply the re-amalgamation technique described in 'The Furniture Doctor', published by Foulsham.

The new lacquer must, of course, match the old in colour, if you are simply patching up, and it is essential to try a 'dummy-run' or two, matching the new lacquer to the old.

This same new lacquer will probably mend small cracks quite as well as any glue. The replacement of structural breaks and missing parts can be built up gradually from very thin layers of plastic wood completely dried in between each layer. Hardened plastic wood can, of course, be sandpapered, and can be scupted if reasonable care is used.

Papier Maché objects are considered highly desirable and well worth collecting, but by the very nature of their construction, they are prone to break and crumble at the edges.

The best repairing agent is epoxy putty, which can be mixed in small quantities. The roughened edges of the papier maché actually help the putty to adhere, and in repairing holes, you can either fill the actual hole with putty, or by making a neat patch repair using thick cardboard cut to fill the missing shape, and fastened into position with epoxy putty, smeared well up on all sides, and at the back and front of the piece.

The techniques of repainting are, of course, identical with the repainting of china.

To complete all processes outlined in Chapter 8, you will need the following tools and materials:

Epoxy glue
Turpentine
Diamond dust, silicon carbide or other abrasive powder

Sandpaper
Choice of fillers
Set of files
Triangular files
Small cutting forceps
Steel shaft
Metal fly-wheel
Wooden crosspiece
Heavy braided nylon fishing line
Copper tubing
Sharp knife
Hammer

Drill with tungsten carbide bit, or core drill

Chapter 8   Unexpected Bonuses

THIS IS not only a chapter of amusing ideas, but of further interesting exercises. After the apprentice pieces of an earlier chapter, these suggest that the sky's the limit, showing that, with a very little imagination, broken or woefully unattractive pieces can be changed into some more useful, or more to one's individual taste.

No matter what antique dealers might say about the value of this and that, no person with any innate taste is going to automatically equate price with beauty, and we all have our particular porcelain *Bêtes Noires*. Faced with the repair of such a piece, we can put our imaginations to work to change it into something more to our own taste.

Thus . . . a slender vase cluttered with ears and handles can become an uncluttered slender vase, possibly of beautiful proportions, if the ears and excrescences are filed off, the sites smoothed with sand-paper, and touched up to match the body. (Cover the sites with a touch of filler if necessary.)

Thus . . . an ungainly jug, the upper part badly damaged, can become a handsome goblet if cut down to the half-way line, or wherever its proportions suggest. You can gild the rim for good measure. You will have to use a drill for the cutting-down operation. (See later in this chapter.)

Thus . . . a teapot of good round shape without spout or handle can be built up, with a little moulding, into a lidded jar, always a curiously expensive item, to hold tea, tobacco, pot pourri, or your life's savings.

Of course it isn't all done by wishing and a dab of cement. To cut down an existing piece through the actual body you are going to need, in addition to patience and a set of fine files, a drill with tungsten carbide bits, or a core drill, which we will describe later. But many other good conversions can be made without this eqiupment.

However, the making and use of the simple drill we describe is not beyond the skill of even the inexperienced, although the psychological block that some of us may put up at the mention of even this simple branch of technology may prevent us from appreciating the art of china repair to the full. (Simple drilling is a requirement of dowelling.)

The list of possible conversions is endless, and it would take far too much book-space to name them all. If you have an eye for the job, the shape of one object will suggest the shape of another, and if it does not, this chapter is not really written for you.

But be warned – once you start on this conversion lark, you'll find it fascinating, and no piece of china in the house will be safe from you, because you will be able to visualize it as being far more interesting in another shape. Better go hunting during the jumble sale season, especially if you are married, and your conjugal partner prefers the household china as it is. The cutting down of all the jugs into soup bowls may give you aesthetic satisfaction, but it may lead to Total Breakdown of Marriage, for which the author takes no responsibility whatsoever.

Riveted Pieces

This is possibly more of a repair than a conversion, but it is possible to remove an unsightly row of rivets from a nice piece, to fill in the rivet holes, and to glue the portions together with epoxy glue, according to instructions already given.

There are three methods of removing rivets:

a) Lever them out carefully with a sharp-pointed tool of some tensile strength.

b) File them through with a small triangular file, and pull the two pieces out with small pliers or forceps.

c) Cut through them with small cutting forceps, obtainable second-hand from your dentist.

The third method is, of course, by far the quickest, but the other two can be quite successful, if tedious.

Riveted pieces, because of the unsightliness of the actual rivets, usually sell very cheaply. The exercise is well worth the trouble.

New lamps for (practically) nothing

Not everything makes a good lamp, no matter what the lamp fiends may say. But a great many china pieces, trimmed down or in their original state, do make lamps of a type that would be very expensive to buy already assembled.

Currently the vase-to-lamp conversion is made extremely easy by the method of inserting a special plug into the *top* of the piece, where it trails a flex down the side, often knocking the shade sideways, and unbalancing the whole lamp to such a degree that it is in constant danger of being knocked over. (It's really only forgiveable when the lamp base is of such a value that it is desirable for it to be kept intact.)

Far the best way is to drill a hole through the bottom of the base, and to make a groove in the stand, if stand there is, to take the flex comfortably, safely and unobtrusively.

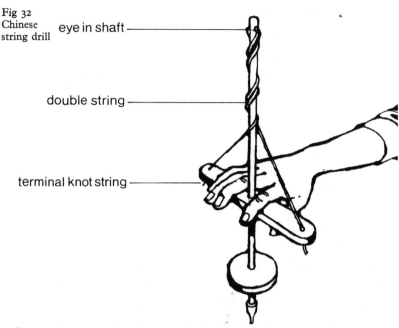

Fig 32
Chinese
string drill

eye in shaft

double string

terminal knot string

Once again, you will need your drill with the tungsten carbide bits, or a diamond bit, which is not as expensive as you might think. You may like to construct the traditional (but never bettered) Chinese String Drill, originally used to drill holes for rivets.

Chinese String Drill
The advantage of this rather archaic apparatus is that it does not bear down as heavily as an electric drill, and although the operation is swift enough, it is not forceful enough to break the porcelain. The making of the String Drill should present no problem to readers conversant with the basic principles of the use of drills, and the above diagram will be of service.

a) Take a metal shaft (preferably steel), length 12–14 inches, diameter $\frac{5}{16}$th of an inch.

b) Taper the shaft towards the top, and make a smooth eye at the tapered end. (Or have a metal worker do it for you.)

c) Take an accurately balanced metal flywheel that fits the shaft, of 8 oz in weight. (The Chinese used a wooden flywheel, but they were experts in overcoming technical disadvantages.) Place it in position as shown in the diagram.

d) Fit a wooden cross piece as shown in the diagram.

e) Fit a small drill-chuck to the bottom end of the shaft.

f) Take a heavy braided nylon fishing line and thread it through the eye, knotting the ends through the terminal holes in the cross piece.

This drill operates quite simply, the cord unwinding in response to hand-pressure on the cross-piece, causing rotation of the drill bit. In spite of the archaic appearance of the drill, the use of a modern drill-chuck enables modern drill-bits to be used.

Core Drilling

This is a system for drilling large holes, and is quite feasible, but extremely tedious. It involves the use of diamond dust or fine silicon carbide or other abrasive powder.

a) Take a short length of copper tubing of the desired diameter, and level off one edge of it very carefully.

b) Nick the cutting end all round with a sharp stout knife lightly tapped with a hammer. Make your nicks of equal length, about half an inch deep.

c) Mix your abrasive powder with a little oil, and rub it well into the nicks.

d) Carefully bend the nicks inwards on themselves without spoiling the shape of the tubing, using some round instrument of slightly smaller diameter than that of the tube itself.

e) Rotate the tube between the palms of the hand, using water or turpentine as a cutting fluid.

f) As the drill begins to cut, add more abrasive to the cut circle. Well, we did warn that it would be a tedious process!

Drilling large holes is properly a job for a drill press, and the shaft can, of course, be fitted to any suitable drill normally used for tungsten carbide bits.

If you are not attracted to the Chinese String drill, there are other satisfactory drills for porcelain. These include the 'egg-beater' drill and the bob-drill, which may not be readily obtainable in your local 'do-it-yourself' shop. Drill manufacturers may be able to help.

There is, of course, nothing in the world against trying any drill that you may have on hand, including electric drills, but it is as well to try them on spare pieces of china first. There are so many types of drill, and so many different porcelain compositions that it is impossible to generalize with any degree of safety. If we appear over-cautious, it does constitute a major tragedy when a good piece is shattered by incorrect drilling, and the author doesn't relish being considered party to it.

To complete all the processes outlined in this book, you will need the following tools and materials:

From a wholesale or retail chemist

Acetone (nail polish remover)
Surgical spirit
Carbon Tetrachloride (dry cleaning fluid)
Plaster of Paris
Powdered whiting
Powdered zinc, tin or titanium oxide
Amyl acetate
Sodium silicate
Powdered glass
Kaolin powder
Alum
Low-melting-point paraffin wax
Beeswax
Carnuba Wax

From a hardware store or do-it-yourself shop

Lacquer thinners
Lacquer or polyurethane coating
Clear varnish
Shellac
Turpentine
Powdered size
Epoxy glue
Uhu glue
Linseed oil
Fine wire brush or steel wool
Sand (or from a pet shop)
Methylated spirits

White spirit
Slender nails
Stiff brass wire or brass nails
Dowel rods
Strips of wooden lath
Small square of glass or glazed tile
Sand-paper or wet-and-dry paper
Porcelain filler
Car touch-up paint
Bronze powders
Small abrasive wheel
Tungsten drill bits
Diamond dust, silicon carbide or other abrasive powders

From an art suppliers or modeller's supply shop

Modelling wax
Plasticine
Barbola
Tubes of water colour
Tubes of oil colour
Casein tempera
Gold paint
American Treasure Gold
Gold leaf (or from a picture restorer)
Special varnish for same
Picture varnish
Tracing paper
Set of artists' brushes
Gold or steel nib
Permanent colour inks
Candle dyes
Small modelling tools
Flexible mould-making material

From a tool-maker or metal worker

Steel shaft
Metal flywheel
Copper tubing

Sports store

Braided nylon fishing line

From your dentist, or a dental supply house

Fine tweezers
Small pointed tool
Fine probe
Small scalpel
Fine cutting forceps
Paribar
Tooth-fillers

Miscellaneous (found in most homes)

Bland soap powder or liquid or soft soap
Clothes pegs
Hammer
Rubber bands
Stout thread or dental floss
Cardboard
Box, tin or wooden block
Indian Muslin
Soft pencil
Button-hook or crochet hook
egg cups or small bowls
Scissors
Knife
2 pairs small pliers
Small file
Small triangular file
Small clamp
Lace or net
Stiff bristled brush
Soft brush
Tape measure

It is also advisable to have a magnifying glass on a stand, or a jewellers'
eye-piece, as china repairing often involves very close work.

The chemicals listed here are usually only required in very small quantities,
and a minimum should be bought, as many deteriorate with keeping.

If you experience any difficulties in finding suppliers, your local Yellow Pages will be a great help. If there are no suppliers in your area, you are almost certain to find what you are looking for in the London directory, or in that of other large commercial centres.

Chapter 9   Turning the Hobby
to Profits

ONCE YOU HAVE REACHED a certain level of expertise, up to the standard of being able to rebuild missing parts of figurines, and to colour and glaze them, you will be quite competent to start your own small business, either to maintain it as a part-time paying hobby, or to build it up into a thriving little enterprise, as you feel inclined.

If this sounds too sanguine and optimistic a judgement, you must remember that professional china repairers are at a premium today, and have become rather choosy as to what type of repair they will undertake, being in a position to do so. If you start with small jobs, you intefere with nobody, and take trade from nobody, and in time you may even be given commissions by overworked experts.

This is, of course, the sort of business in which you 'start small', but it is also a business in which your capital outlay is minimal, and your workroom can be an undisturbed corner of your own home. (There are Council regulations regarding working at home, which should be checked on, but such enterprises usually receive sympathetic hearings from the various authorities.)

Necessary equipment
In addition to the equipment outlined in this book, you will need a work bench, or failing this, the best thing you can do is to search through second-hand furniture shops for the large heavy type of dining room table, usually with draw leaves, which went out of fashion with six-children families. If the surface is worn and scored (which won't matter in the slightest, because it will probably become further scratched during use), you may be lucky enough to get one very cheaply.

But do avoid a veneered top, unless you are prepared to peel off the whole of the veneer, because over a period of time it will lift and 'bump up', and give you an uneven surface. Make sure that the table is completely steady. If it has a short leg or two, this is better dealt with by putting a square of hardboard or even cardboard under the offending legs, rather than trying to shorten the longer ones, which is seldom satisfactory unless you are prepared to shave down cross-grained wood, always a tedious exercise. If the tenon joints joining the legs to the table top are loose, they can be glued back into place with Araldite. Turn the table upside down during the process.

Choose a chair of exactly the right height . . . not a stool, because any kind of sitting-down work requires a back rest. By 'correct height' we mean one which allows you to rest your elbows comfortably on your work top while actually working. Wooden blocks will bring a suitable chair up to the correct height.

(If we seem to be advocating a penny pinching programme in this enterprise, it is because we firmly believe that a business which will, in the first instance, bring in small returns, should keep its initial expenses as low as possible, or too long a time will pass before you break even. And this would represent an unsound business principle.)

Further to this, you will need as large a set of shelves as you can obtain, to separate work to be done, completed work awaiting collection, and work in various stages of repair.

For some reason best known to furniture manufacturers, shelf-sets seem to be among the most expensive articles of furniture, but you can get round this problem by watching for shops closing down prior to demolition, or are under-going refitting, and disposing of their rather old fashioned fittings.

A friend of mine obtained a 10 foot long brass and plate glass counter from a gents' outfitters, which had three tiers of wooden pull-out box drawers (in mahogany, incidentally), *absolutely free* 'for the taking-away', as the saying goes. The taking-away was not a easy job, because it was immensely heavy, but the only cost was £2 for the hire of a small van, and beer for the four friends who solemnly carried this immense prize out of the shop. It is possibly a monstrous piece of furniture, but it is the nucleus of his workshop, as he not only has space to store pieces in various stages of repair, but also has a plate glass working top as well.

In addition to these essentials, we add two more. If you do not normally use a jewellers' glass or a magnifying glass on a stand when repairing china, you would be well advised to get one, because a great deal of close work can be trying to the eyes. Your other requirement is an adjustable desk lamp which throws light directly onto your hands and your work. An adjustable goose neck lamp, or one with a jointed stem is ideal.

Shop or work shop
It might not be viable for you to work at home (or regulations may forbid it), in which case you will have to consider renting suitable premises. The first thing to remember is that you are not intending to run a boutique or restaurant, and you do not need to put up a 'front'. The amount of what is termed 'off the street' trade that you would gain by positioning yourself in an expensive High Street position will be minimal, and a high rent will throw a great financial strain on a small business. The 'better mouse trap' which you are

hoping to build will, attract its own clientele in its own good time, if you follow the advertising plan which we suggest. If people know where you are, they will seek you out when they need their china repaired.

Therefore, if you want to rent a shop or work shop at a minimal rent, you will do as well in areas where trade trends have changed, and commerce has gone elsewhere. Admittedly these areas have run down a bit, and the shops usually need a fair amount of redecorating, but a couple of pots of paint can work wonders, and often these premises are neglected simply because they are too small for modern retail commerce, but of exactly the right size for a china repair business. Such shops are often let for as little as £2 a week (which usually means that some repair is necessary), and are usually on a weekly or monthly tenancy, with no deposit required, as might be in more expensive premises. To be really on the safe side, you must be prepared to start out with sufficient capital to pay your rent and other expenses for at least 3 months.

The best course is to visit all available estate agents, stating your case quite clearly and simply and frankly. Don't be afraid to say quite firmly that you are looking for cheap premises. Snubs are very few, and any agent worth his salt will have an eye to letting you better premises later when you have built up a viable little business. (If you rent a shop, regulations usually forbid you to use it exclusively as a work shop. You must sell *something*. The making of lamps and the selling of them is a viable proposition, or you can sell bric-a-brac on a commission basis for various clients, in which case you need no capital outlay.)

Canvassing for customers

Well now, we will presume that you have set yourself up in premises, either in your own home, or in rented premises. And there you sit, drumming your fingers on your work top, wondering what your next move should be.

The next move is to find a jobbing printer and to get 100 business cards printed, at an approximate cost of £1.50. These should be small and neat, and should give your name and address, the words 'China Repairs' or something similar, and your telephone number if you have one. (A telephone is highly desirable, and if you don't already have one, you should consider it a first priority. You can run a successful business without one, but you'll have to do a great deal more walking.)

Armed with your business cards, and with two or three examples of your best repairs, visit every single antique dealer in your town, or, if you live in a city, in your own area, extending that area week by week. Do each antique dealer the courtesy of calling only when he is not busy, which probably means *not* on a Saturday, and not on market day. If he appears co-operative, that is, prepared to recommend you to his customers, or to commission you to do repairs for him, leave your card, and subsequently telephone him at regular intervals.

Keep a note-book detailing places where cards have been left, the telephone of the shop concerned, and any particular details with regard to suitable times for phoning, calling etc.

After you have tackled the antique shops, call in turn on every shop which sells china of any type, including department stores with china sections. Ask to see the manager, or, in the case of the department stores, the buyer. If the individual you want is not available, try to make an appointment. They may not have direct work for you, but often customers bring back broken china and may very well be referred to you for repairs.

Modern china, especially dinner, tea and coffee sets, can be divided in 'stock patterns', i.e. those in which broken pieces can be replaced, and 'non stock patterns', in which case the pattern has either been discontinued or is 'one off' and no replacements are available. In the latter two cases, there is often scope for a china repairer.

Your third step is to write or type cards (post-card size) and have one placed in as many newsagents windows, for about 5p a week, as are within walking distance. These newsagents are usually kind obliging people, and, failing a telephone number on your part, may well take messages for you from potential clients.

A small box advertisement in the classified columns of your local paper may bring good results, but it should be continuous, because it seldom makes an impact on anyone who hasn't actually got broken china needing mending. When this occurs, such a person may vaguely remember having seen an advertisement in the local paper, but can't remember the address. If a glance at the current issue of the local paper doesn't reveal the information, a potential customer is lost.

If you have a telephone, you can have it registered as a business phone, for an addition fee of £1. This entitles you to an entry in the Yellow Pages of the telephone directory at no extra cost. If there are no other china repairers in your directory, you have the right for your name and address to appear under that heading, even if yours is the only name. The make-up of the Yellow Pages is under the direction of the firm of Thomsons, whose local address will be found in the Yellow Pages of your local telephone directory.

Another form of advertising that you may care to try is the use of what is known in the printing trade as 'dodgers', small single sheet handbills, which can be printed by your local jobbing printer at a cost of about £3.50 a hundred. These can be slipped through the letter boxes in various houses, and you will be very unlucky indeed if this doesn't bring in some response.

Once you have established your contacts, your Golden Rule should be that these contacts must be maintained on a regular basis. That is to say, if you cannot phone these antique shops and china shops and the newsagents, you should at least put your head in at the door at least once a week, to see if they have any work for you.

What to charge

This is probably the most difficult paragraph in the whole of this chapter, because there are a great many factors to be considered, including the fact that you will probably start out mending the type of china no longer dealt with by the experts, because its intrinsic value is comparatively low. Obviously one does not charge more for a repair than the value of the article, and usually, at the start of a small business, one cannot pass up even the humblest job.

It is, however, advisable to make a minimum charge, or you are going to be bogged down in paper work for very little return, because the paper work involved in a job equals that of gluing of a single saucer for one customer or repairing six pieces for another. (Oh, yes, there's always paper work.)

Therefore, if you set your minimum charge at, say, 25p or 50, and the job is a simple gluing repair, and if this seems a bit rich for your client's blood, you could offer to do another repair (or other repairs) within the same charge.

A multiple plate repair, especially if there are holes to fill in, is worth at least 50p, if it's ordinary domestic china, and it is unlikely that the customer will be willing to pay more than half the value of a new piece.

More complicated repairs can be assessed on the amount of time the repair takes, and this will mean that you will have to decide in your own mind how much to charge on hour. (In assessing your time, the drying time cannot be counted, because this leaves you free to carry on with another job.) Until you become really expert, and therefore reasonably swift in working, you may be wise to pitch your hourly rate fairly low, possibly as low as 30p an hour, bearing in mind that when you get a proper speed up, you should be able to make £1 an hour, without increasing your charge to your customers.

It is also accepted business practice to work on domestic china for a reasonable low rate, and to quote a higher *pro rata* price for more expensive pieces. This does not mean that your cheaper jobs should be of lower quality than your more expensive ones. Simple business ethics would dictate against this practice, and in any case, your personal reputation would certainly suffer. As you build up your business, you can drop off the cheaper jobs if you want to.

You will have to learn to quote the price for a job, as many customers like to know what the charge will be when they bring in a piece for repair. This is better done if, as soon as you have any idea in your mind that you might like to start a china repair business, to start you keep a statistical record, describing every repair you do, and timing yourself as accurately as possible. This will be invaluable to you when you do actually start working commercially, because nothing is more unbusinesslike than giving a quote to a customer, and then increasing the cost when the customer comes to collect the repair.

It is far too tedious to try to assess the cost of materials used in each individual repair, particularly as they are usually used in infinitesimal amounts. It is better to add an over-all charge for materials, e.g. for simple repairs, 5 per cent, and for more complicated repairs, in which there is rebuilding of parts, 10 per cent. If you use gilding, especially gold leaf, you could set the percentage at 12 or 15.

Do not itemize these expenses to a customer, even if you submit an invoice. Simply quote a firm price, and leave it at that.

If all this sounds rather complicated, it very quickly becomes second nature to look at a potential repair, and know with accuracy how long it is going to take you, how much of which materials you are going to use, and the value of the piece. Thus the price of the repair will come into your mind automatically, and finally you won't even have to think about it.

Keeping books

No matter what business enterprise you care to undertake, you must keep a careful check on your incoming and outgoing expenses. Even if you run the business at a loss, you must be aware of the amount of loss, and this is not only for your own personal benefit, but for the benefit of the Department of Inland Revenue.

An essential expenditure, before you take your first repair, is to buy a simple ledger from any stationers, and to open it at its first double page. At the top of the left page, write the word 'Debit', and at the top of the right page 'Credit'.

On your Debit page, write down every single penny that you pay out, with the date, the item and the amount. (You will find a date column on the left margin, and money columns on the right.) 'Every single penny' means exactly that . . . every postage stamp, every pound of plaster of Paris, every mug for your work time coffee break. Put down *everything*. If anything is disallowed for income tax purposes, it will be taken out without prejudice, and it is far more difficult to add items later for purposes of rebate after your books have been made up. And put every item down *at once*, because small items are easy to forget.

On your Credit page, you write down, of course, all moneys paid in to you. By the very nature of the business, you will have far more debit items than credits, although it is to be hoped that within a short space of time, the *amount* (but not necessarily the *number*) of credits will exceed your debits, and then you will be running your business at a profit.

When you reach the bottom of the page, add up both your debit and credit pages, and carry the amount over onto the top of the next page, with the words 'Brought Forward', and the amount.

Balance your books every month, i.e. add up your debits and credits, rule right across the page, and start again for the next month. If in the early stages of the business, things don't look too bright, it is as well to know it, because if you are going to worry, better worry about existing facts, than to let your imagination run riot and think that things are worse than they really are.

If you are unlucky enough to have a debit/credit gap, it is a great help to look at your monthly balance, and see that the gap is narrowing month by month . . . as it almost always does in a china repairer's business. It is in the early stages that you will be thankful that you didn't put a deal of capital into your fine looking High Street shop.

Remember, in the early stages, that every debit reduces your income tax liability (keep *every* invoice and receipt, and if the suppliers of your materials don't normally give them, they will if you insist), and nobody pays tax on a loss.

If all this seems a little pernickety in a small business that's just starting, remember that the business will grow, and it's never too soon to form these good business habits, which are a requirement by law, in any case.

Even if your business, in its early stages, may not justify the attentions of a qualified accountant, you will find that your local branch of the Inland Revenue is not completely staffed by tea drinking ogres, no matter what you may have heard to the contrary. If you work at home, you will find that you are possibly entitled to unexpected benefits, such as a rebate on part of your rent, and on your telephone. If you use a typewriter, you can claim a rebate on its upkeep. A chat with someone at your local branch may reveal unexpected bonuses.

Modus operandi

When a customer brings in an article for repair, the article must immediately be marked indelibly to identify it, but in such a way that the mark can be removed when it is returned to the customer.

The best way to do this is to enter the transaction in a numbered book, giving the customer's name and address, a description of the piece, and some indication of the repair to be effected. Then write the number of the repair on the bottom of the piece in *nail polish* of a contrasting colour to the piece itself. Labels tend to detach themselves, but the nail polish mark can remain on the piece until it is claimed by the customer, when it can easily be removed with a piece of cotton wool soaked in remover.

Always have a special place for articles awaiting repair, and another, quite separate, for those awaiting collection, and these places should be on shelves, where there is no danger of their being dislodged. You are responsible for these pieces while they are in your possession, and should take every care with them. To display a notice disclaiming responsibility may absolve you legally, but such a notice does not conjure up the type of china repairer who is likely to inspire confidence in the mind of a potential customer. There are classic stories of Ming vases shattered to pieces by repairers and put together without a single trace of the disaster, but this represents a great deal of wasted time, if nothing else.

Keep a receipt book, in case a customer should want one. There is no need to give a receipt to every single customer (provided you write the amount down in the Credit column of your ledger), because the custom of writing a receipt for every customer is normally only used where there are employees . . . and you are your own boss.

You will certainly need a 'float', that is, a sum of money from which you can give change to a customer. This money does not figure in your ledger, because it is neither debit nor credit, and it is as well to remember its existence when you count your daily takings, lest you get over excited at having had such a good day. The amount of this float is at your own discretion, but you should be able to give change for £5 if required.

If your takings begin to accrue, you would be wise not to leave them on the premises overnight. Most banks have night safes in which you can slip your takings on the way home, and the possession of a cheque account (or a separate one if you already have a personal one), is a great help in business.

If you work from shop or workshop, do try to maintain regular hours, because nothing annoys a customer as much as finding a shop closed when it is expected to be open. Prepare a card and place it in your window stating your business hours, and then stick to those hours as far as possible, or arrange for the owner of some other small shop to take in repairs in your absence. Irregular hours will not only lose you the specific customer who calls and finds your premises closed, but may lose you further custom, because the tale that you are 'never open' will soon circulate, and people may not want to travel the distance simply in the hope of finding you available. In other words, if you offer a service, you must render that service to your very best ability. This is how a sound little business is built up.

A number of businesses these days close at lunch time, and the choice of staying open or closing is, of course, up to you, provided you post a clear notice in your window to inform customers of the fact. If you are not accustomed to business life, you might be wise to give yourself an hour's break at mid-day, not only to have a decent meal, but also to walk around a bit, and get the cricks out of neck and back after unaccustomed sitting. (There is also shopping to consider.) If these points don't bother you, and you decide to 'work through', do make provision for a good sandwich lunch, and the where-withall to make a cup of coffee or tea. It is usually possible for a nearby café or restaurant to send in a lunch tray on a regular basis, and if you are in the kind of area where rents are reasonable, don't automatically discount the 'Joe's Cafe' type of place, because the food is often quite good and reasonably priced, even if it is chips with everything, served on china of the type that you wouldn't think of repairing, even in your apprentice days.

Finally, don't neglect to provide yourself with wrapping paper, tissue paper, string and cellotape. Each returned repair should be neatly and securely packed. If you are required to send a delicate piece through the post, you will need to do better. Go to your local shoe shop, and ask for empty shoe boxes, which they will have in plenty, because few customers seem to want the boxes along with their new shoes. (You will, of course, need smaller boxes for smaller pieces. Various people in various trades throw out cardboard boxes of all sizes, and they can be had for the asking.) After wrapping your piece in tissue paper, you must fill the remaining box space with some substance which has a certain amount of 'give', to absorb shock. The most obvious is wood wool, called by the Americans 'Excelsior', which again can usually be had for the asking, especially as the amount you require will be relatively small. Alter-natives . . . vermiculite, which is used in house insulation, and looks like a particularly horrible breakfast food . . . foam rubber chips, which are used for stuffing cushions . . . and, believe it or not, plain (not sugar-covered) popcorn. In fact, the latter is the best of the lot. Cram your box with popcorn, and you can send the most delicate article around the world without damage. If you post an article, you are, of course, entitled to make a charge for postage and possibly for packing, and if the value of the article warrants it, send it by registered post.

Which brings us to the question of payment. Unless a customer deals with you on a regular basis (or has a well-established business), it is not advisable to extend credit. Quite honest people can be careless about small debts, and the chasing up of outstanding accounts is both time consuming and un-pleasant. There is nothing wrong with explaining that you run a strictly cash business.

Should you accept cheques? This is a difficult problem at a time when cheque frauds are on the increase, and when so many people appear to be increasingly careless with their cheque books, to the extent that they fall into the wrong hands. On the other hand, where an individual is accustomed to dealing by cheque, offence may be cause by refusing to accept the practice.

Actually, a small business such as this is unlikely to be the target for cheque con-artists, who usually go into larger shops and obtain goods by these fraudu-lent means, but should you be asked to accept a cheque, it is an acceptable business practice to ask the customer to show proof of identity, which does *not* mean a letter from Auntie Maud asking her over for Sunday dinner, but a Banker's card or other document which shows the actual signature. Then watch the customer write the signature on the cheque, which is the surest indication of the ownership of the cheque book, because signatures are normally scrawled almost automatically, and slow careful writing *could* be a sign that the name is unfamiliar to the writer.

If you are in real doubt, ask for the loan of the cheque book while you telephone the bank concerned. If you then disappear into a back room, you may well return to find your customer gone, and you with a stolen cheque book in your hand.

Should a customer ask for change from a cheque, i.e. the permission to make out a larger cheque than is needed to pay for the repair, so that she can have spending money, to save her the trouble of calling at the bank, it is usually better, in a small business, to say that you don't have sufficient in the till to oblige her in this matter, which will probably be true, anyway, because you do always need as much change as possible. The acceptance of a cheque may tie up your money for as much as a week, while the cheque is cleared, and this is not a good business principle, especially in the early stages.

We have dealt with this matter of building up a china repair business at some length, possibly to the extent of tedium to those who already possess some knowledge of business procedure, because this is an excellent trade for people who, for various reasons, have never had the opportunity to engage in any sort of commerce before.

China repairing is a most suitable occupation for those whose movements are limited by their own health or disabilities, or the health or disabilities of near relatives.

One needs, of course, good eye-sight and the full use of one's hands, but an individual confined to a wheel chair can build up a very lucrative business in this field, although it is desirable to have someone else to help with the leg-work, which is not indispensible, but which helps to build up the business a little faster. A post-coronary patient, forbidden by the doctor to return to the 'rat race', can adjust his working hours according to his daily state of his health, and can certainly, and possibly in a surprisingly short time, make an income almost comparable with his previous one, without the slightest stress. There is something very soothing about china repairing.

One can even, if one is a tidy worker, repair china in bed, if one is confined in this way. The necessities . . . a large bed tray, with a built up edge to confine one's materials on the tray (one doesn't really want Barbola crumbs between the sheets), and a handy shelf on which to place one's supported and finished pieces.

(The authors of this book would be extremely interested whether it is possible for people using arm hoists to repair china. In considering china repairing to be a very suitable occupation for the disabled, they would like to explore the therapeutic possibilities to the fullest possible extent.)

Where an individual is confined at home to nurse aged or ill relatives, china repairing can form the ideal occupation, because, as we have already explained, the work can be carried on at home, and is actually one of the most lucrative of the home industries. One is seldom in a position where work cannot be left for a few minutes, and it is surprising how much of the work can be done even by elderly and disabled people, who are often glad of the occupation, and the participation in a viable financial project.

There are societies dealing with various types of disability, and with the problems encountered by people house bound because of the needs of others. Some of them provide financial help for the starting of projects such as this, and it is well worth while enquiring into the matter.